THE QUR'ĀN IN SIXTEENTH-CENTURY SPAIN: SIX MORISCO VERSIONS OF SŪRA 79

CONSUELO LOPEZ-MORILLAS

THE QUR'ĀN IN SIXTEENTH-CENTURY SPAIN: SIX MORISCO VERSIONS OF SŪRA 79

TAMESIS BOOKS LIMITED
LONDON

Colección Támesis
SERIE A - MONOGRAFIAS, LXXXII

I. S. B. N.: 0-7293-0121-4.

Depósito Legal: M. 20.079 - 1982.
Printed in Spain by Imprenta Aguirre
for
TAMESIS BOOKS LIMITED
LONDON

To my mother and father.

CONTENTS

		Pages
	Acknowledgements	11
I.	Introduction	13
II.	Language of the texts	27
III.	Tafsīr	47
IV.	The texts	57
V.	Glossary	83
VI.	Photographs of the texts	97
VII.	Bibliography and abbreviations	99

Acknowledgements.

Many teachers, colleagues, and friends have guided and assisted me since I first began to study the Aljamiado Qur'ān. I wish to thank most particularly Professors James T. Monroe and Yakov Malkiel of the University of California at Berkeley, the first for opening up to me the riches of Hispano-Arabic literature, and the second for directing my doctoral studies and providing the strong linguistic foundation necessary to pursue them. Juan Vernet Ginés of the University of Barcelona has been generous in sharing information about manuscripts and about work in progress by him and his students. I have profited greatly from conversations with my former colleague, Professor Michael J. Zwettler of the Ohio State University. Ms. Gail Trecker, while a student at Ohio State, made the initial transliteration of the J 39 manuscript. And Professor Jerry R. Craddock of Berkeley, after reading large portions of the manuscript in draft form, made valuable suggestions for its improvement.

This work could not even have been begun without access to the major libraries and manuscript collections in which the source materials are housed. My thanks go to the following persons and institutions: Don Fernando de la Granja Santamaría of the Instituto Miguel Asín (Escuela de Estudios Arabes), Consejo Superior de Investigaciones Científicas, Madrid; the Biblioteca Nacional, Madrid; Doña Julia Méndez Aparicio, librarian of the Biblioteca Pública Provincial, Toledo; and Mesdemoiselles Marie-Rose Séguy and Yvette Sauvan of the section of Oriental manuscripts, Bibliothèque Nationale, Paris.

My research has been supported at various stages by generous grants from the American Association of University Women, the College of Humanities of the Ohio State University, the American Council of Learned Societies, and the President's Council of International Programs of Indiana University.

Finally, I wish to acknowledge the unfailing support of my husband, Enrique Merino Muedra, who has had to live with the Aljamiado Qur'ān as long as he has lived with me, but who shows no signs of getting tired of either of us.

Bloomington, Indiana, July 1980.

I. INTRODUCTION.

On the second of May in the year 1606, somewhere in Spain —perhaps in one of the *aljamas* or Morisco quarters of the larger towns— a Spanish Muslim is performing a labor of love and piety: he is copying a translation of the Qur'ān. He has completed a quarter of the book; he pauses to make a note of that fact on the manuscript. Then, moved perhaps by a need to justify himself before his fellow Muslims, he extends his notation to two full pages: writing in a mixture of Spanish, Aljamiado, and Arabic, he begs his readers' indulgence for his task:

> Ešta eškrito en letra de krištyanoš ... rruega y suplica que por eštar en dicha letra no lo tengan en menoš de lo keš, anteš en mucho; porque pues esta asi declarado, esta mas a vista de los muçlimes que saben leer el *cris*tiano y no la letra de los muçlimes. Porq*ue* es cierto q*ue* dixo el annabī Muḥammad *ṣallā Allahu ᶜalayhi wa-sallam* ke la mejor lengwa era la ke še entendia.

"It is written in the letters of the Christians: [the writer] begs that on account of being in those letters it not be belittled, but rather respected; because, being set down in this way, it can better be seen by those Muslims who know how to read Christian, but not Muslim, letters. For it is true that the Prophet Muḥammad (peace be upon him) said that the best language was the one that could be understood" [1].

The unknown scribe had every reason to feel apologetic, since he knew that in translating the Qur'ān he was violating one of the tenets of his faith. Muslims everywhere and in all ages have been charged with reading and reciting their scripture in Arabic, whatever their native speech. But this Muslim knew not only that there was a clear need for a Spanish Qur'ān in his community, but that in preparing his version he was merely continuing a tradition begun exactly one hundred fifty years before, in 1456. In that year was made the first known translation of the entire Qur'ān into Spanish.

The circumstances of that first version have been amply explored and described by Darío Cabanelas [2] and need be summarized only briefly here. The reverend father Juan de Segovia, realizing that any polemic against Islam must be based upon a solid understanding of its doctrines, sought out the two existing Latin versions of the Qur'ān and suspected —though he was ignorant of Arabic— that both were sadly lacking in accuracy. He took upon himself, therefore, the task of commissioning a Spanish translation of the work. To that end he persuaded a respected *faqīh* from Toledo, ᶜĪsā ibn Jābir, to travel to distant Savoy, where Juan was at the time in the service of the local ruler. Over a period of four winter months ᶜĪsā, by working diligently, completed the translation of the Qur'ān and added to it a commentary based on Arabic sources. He then returned to his post in the *mudéjar* community of Toledo, leaving Juan to flesh out his Spanish translation with a parallel Latin version —the whole forming "the first trilingual Qur'ān" of Cabanelas' title.

Sadly for the study of Spanish Islam and for our present investigations, ᶜĪsā's translation is no longer extant. Yet far from disappearing without a trace, it may well have served as the inspiration, if not actually the direct model, for all subsequent translations made by Muslims for as long as they continued to occupy Spanish soil: until 1609, a bare three years after the writer in our opening paragraphs defended the practice of putting the Qur'ān into "letra de krištyanoš".

Less than forty years after this Spanish translation of 1456 was made, the Christian Reconquest of Granada profoundly altered the circumstances of Muslims all over Spain. Now known as Moriscos [3], they were the object of unrelenting religious and social oppression: forced to accept baptism, denied their ancestral homes and relocated among suspicious "Old Christians", forbidden to educate their children in their faith, they nonetheless clung doggedly to such doctrines and practices of Islam as they were able to preserve. Needless to say, it was the Qur'ān that they cherished above all, but the Arabic Qur'ān grew increasingly inaccessible to them as their educational system was eroded and their worship reduced to a few hurried, clandestine rites. If Islam was to be kept alive among the Moriscos, these Muslim Spaniards would have to be able to read their scripture in their own language. It is at this point that ᶜĪsā's translation may have played a decisive part. Though intended, paradoxically enough, for Christians, that their preachers might attack Islam more convincingly, that first Spanish version may by its very existence have broken the taboo against rendering the Qur'ān into any foreign tongue. Whether the Moriscos actually copied ᶜĪsā's version we shall never know, since it is lost to us. But at least some of the many Morisco Qur'āns from the sixteenth century that have survived could be its spiritual, if not its literal, heirs.

Throughout the sixteenth century, up to the time of their final expulsion in 1609, the Moriscos continued to copy the Arabic Qur'ān and to translate it into Aljamiado. In writing Spanish with Arabic characters they succeeded in preserving at least the outward form of the language in which God had proclaimed His message to mankind. The survival of nearly seventy Morisco Qur'ān MSS into modern times bears witness not only to the abundance of copies which must have been produced —for we may assume that only a fraction escaped destruction— but to the pains which the Moriscos must have taken to ensure their preservation. Many Qur'āns, indeed, have been discovered along with other Aljamiado works in the secret caches to which their owners consigned them and in which they lay hidden for hundreds of years [4].

Virtually all of the extant Qur'āns in Aljamiado are incomplete, in part because of deterioration of the MSS themselves, but chiefly because the Moriscos were wont to select only portions of their scripture to translate, choosing passages appropriate for use in daily prayer. The initial, longer chapters —those corresponding to the Medinan period when Muḥammad was consolidating his community— clearly had scant appeal. Their lengthy prescriptions on such matters as the pilgrimage to Mecca, money-lending, diet, and marriage must have meant little to Muslims who were striving to keep up even a rudimentary semblance of their faith, while surrounded by Christians who hastened to report any suspicious practices to the Inquisition. Thus Sūras 2 through 37 tend to be represented in Aljamiado MSS by only a few isolated verses. In the latter part of the book, however, the chapters are not only briefer and thus inherently more quotable, but their content is of a more inspiring nature. Chronologically the earliest to be revealed, these Sūras of the Meccan period are full of emotional fire: God's message is new and the need to preach it is urgent. In these chapters the promise of Paradise beckons, while the threat of Hell menaces all unbelievers; God is less the law-giver than the Creator, the All-Merciful, yet also the fearsome Judge. It is small wonder that the Moriscos found these passages to be the closest to their own emotional needs. Their lives left little room for complex theology, but they could respond to simple, highly-charged appeals to believe and be saved. The great cataclysm of the Last Judgment —"when the sun shall be darkened, when the stars shall be thrown down" [5]— may even have been associated in their minds with that longed-for day when, as they believed, their coreligionists would invade the Iberian Peninsula, reverse the Christian Reconquest, and return all Spain to the fold of Islam. Therefore it is not unusual to find Morisco Qur'āns which are complete (or intended to be so, though perhaps not perfectly preserved) in Sūras 38 through 114, to which is generally added the *Fātiḥa* or opening prayer.

In recent years these Aljamiado versions of the Qur'ān have begun to be the object of study, chiefly by Juan Vernet of the University of Barcelona and his students. The texts of two MSS have been transliterated and printed in full: J. Vernet and L. Moraleda, "Un Alcorán fragmentario en aljamiado", *BRABLB,* XXXIII (1969-70), 43-75, and J. Vernet and C. López Lillo, "Un manuscrito morisco del Corán", *BRABLB,* XXXV (1973-74), 185-255. The MSS are, respectively, numbers 25 and 18 of the Escuela de Estudios Arabes (Instituto Miguel Asín) in Madrid (they are traditionally known as J 25 and J 18 from the former name of the institute, "Junta para la Ampliación de Estudios"), and they contain the following Qur'ānic passages: (J 25) Sūras 1; 2:2-5, 147-156, 158-163, 255-259, 284-286; 3:2-6, 16-19, 25-27; 9:128-130; 16:98; 18:107-110; 26:78-79; 28:88; 30:16-19; 33:40-44; 36:55; 56:74-96; 59:18-24; 67; 78-114, complete; (J 18): Sūras 41-54, complete; 55:1-4, 13-78; 56, complete.

Vernet's chief aim has been a modest one, to make the texts themselves available in printed form, and he has therefore not added to them any kind of critical or linguistic study, glossary, or other scholarly apparatus. While the mere availability of the texts is welcome, the transliterations themselves are full of small inaccuracies which greatly diminish their usefulness [6].

Also prepared at Barcelona, but unavailable for consultation, are T. Losada Campo, *Estudios sobre Coranes aljamiados* (doctoral dissertation, University of Barcelona, 1975), and M. V. Viscasillas Seguí, *Traducciones aljamiadas del Corán. Estudio lingüístico de unos fragmentos. Manuscrito 25 de la Escuela de Estudios Arabes de Madrid* (licenciate thesis, Autonomous University of Barcelona, 1973) [7].

Seen against the existing literature on the Aljamiado Qur'ān, the present monograph breaks new ground on several counts. The most important is its comparative approach: the juxtaposition of six versions of the same chapter of the Qur'ān illuminates the texts in ways not hitherto possible. Over twenty years have passed since it was first suggested that ᶜĪsā ibn Jābir's translation of 1456 might well have inspired all subsequent Morisco translations [8]. But the unavailability of texts, and especially of different texts of the same Qur'ānic passages, has made it impossible to compare the Aljamiado versions among themselves. Whether there existed a "standard" Aljamiado Qur'ān which later scribes merely reproduced, or whether any capable Morisco could undertake his own translation from the Arabic original, has not been established before now [9]. Our investigations, though based on a very limited sample of all the texts, supply an unequivocal answer to this question.

Furthermore, the present study undertakes a detailed description and analysis of the language of these Qur'ānic texts. While we are already in possession of valuable linguistic studies of Aljamiado, dating back to Menéndez Pidal's pioneering venture of 1902[10], the particular language of the Aljamiado Qur'ān has, as previously stated, remained unexplored. And, almost inevitably, such language must display special characteristics. Not only is translation involved —leading one to expect the normal interference of the source language with the target language— but the text being translated is the object of extraordinary veneration, not only in in its content but in its very means of expression. Such reverence called for a high degree of literalness in the Spanish version. Yet the Moriscos were hampered by their poor command of Arabic, which had become for them, over time, a purely liturgical language, often but imperfectly understood. A close examination of the ways in which they rendered this holiest of Arabic books can tell us much about the Moriscos' grasp of Arabic.

More significantly still, an understanding of the language of these texts provides in most cases the only key to their date and place of origin. In the present group, only one MS explicitly reveals the former, and none the latter. Thus any hope of establishing at least their relative, if not their absolute, chronology lies in the evidence of their language. Most of Aljamiado literature is characterized, linguistically speaking, by two traits: archaism and dialectalism. The first is attributable to the relative isolation of the Moriscos from Spanish society, as well as by the general traditionalism or conservatism inherent in their constant harking back to the Arab domination which had ended in the previous century. The second turns on the fact that the Moriscos were heavily concentrated in non-Castilian-speaking regions of the Peninsula, notably Aragon and Valencia. Both the archaic and the dialectal aspects of Aljamiado, then, provide a gauge by which to estimate the relative ages of a given set of texts; in reality the two work together, since the Aragonese dialect is phonologically more conservative than Castilian. When two MSS which contain essentially the same text differ in certain key phonological or morphological features, it may safely be surmised that one is older than the other or originated in a region of more conservative speech. The implications of this fact for the study of these six Qur'ānic MSS are set forth in full in the section "Language of the Texts".

Finally, the comparative study of several Aljamiado versions of a single chapter of the Qur'ān advances our knowledge of Qur'ānic exegesis as it was practiced among the Moriscos. Many passages of commentary, ranging in length from a single word to a whole paragraph, are incorporated into the translations with the aim of expanding or clarifying the often cryptic Arabic text. These commentaries clearly derive from Arabic works of *tafsīr,* Qur'ānic exegesis. The genre is known to have flourished in Muslim Spain, but since almost no *tafsīr* texts from al-Andalus have survived, it is not known on which of the various authorities the Moriscos depended for their interpretation of scripture. (It is highly unlikely that they created their own original brand of exegesis.) By comparing the Morisco texts with selected works of *tafsīr* in Arabic, from both the East and Arab Spain, we have been able to suggest tentative answers to this question and to point out directions for further exploration.

Approaching the Aljamiado Qur'ān as an object of research —linguistic, historical, cultural, theological— looms as a formidable task, especially as one contemplates the dozens of MSS with their thousands of folios. It seems prudent, then, to select a manageable but representative slice of all the available material and to study it in such a way as to create a model for future investigations. To limit one's texts to a reasonable number and length permits a depth and detail of supporting apparatus which would not be feasible otherwise. At the same time, if small sections of the work are given individual, serious attention, and if the problems of interpretation which occur are resolved a few at a time, a mosaic of such brief studies can be built up, eventually to result in a critical edition of the entire Aljamiado Qur'ān.

The present work seeks to act as just such a model. The portion of the Qur'ān chosen for study is Sūra (chapter) 79, *Sūrat an-Nāziᶜāt* or "The Pluckers", consisting of forty-six verses (the longest chapter of the Qur'ān contains two hundred eighty-six verses, the shortest three). A number of factors determined the choice of this particular Sūra. First, the five initial verses are (like many passages of the Qur'ān) highly elliptical and cryptic, and hence difficult to translate. If we wish to determine how many different Morisco translations of the Qur'ān were in existence, it is useful to examine such passages as these, whose meaning is by no means clear. Should various Aljamiado versions render the verses in essentially the same way, we could assume that the scribes were following some sort of common model. At the same time, the passage in question is one on which exegetes have expended a good deal of ink; the authors of different works of *tafsīr* have speculated on the exact nature of "those that pluck out vehemently" (are they angels?) and "those that swim serenely" (could they be ships?). If the Moriscos followed a variety of commentarists on the Qur'ān, the differing opinions of the latter on verses 1-5 should be reflected in the Aljamiado versions.

A second reason for the choice of Sūra 79 as a model text is that it incorporates, in verses 15 to 25, part of the story of Moses —specifically, the episode in which God commands Moses to carry His message to Pharaoh. As may be assumed from its appearance in both Jewish and Muslim scripture, Moses' story must have had considerable appeal for the Semitic peoples; the patriarch is in fact mentioned on over thirty separate occasions in the Qur'ān. Such a popular account would, like all popular narratives, be subject to frequent retelling and thus to varying degrees of elaboration. If we assume that Arabic *tafsīr*-writers might have incorporated different versions of the legend into their commentaries, we may be able to follow the varying lines of exegesis into the Aljamiado texts as a way of classifying these into related groups.

Finally, Sūra 79 has been selected as a representative chapter on purely thematic grounds: its final third (verses 34-36) consists of a vivid prediction of how mankind will be judged on the Last Day. The vision of the Apocalypse seems to have gained an especially powerful hold on the Moriscos' imagination, and similar passages are common among the portions of the Qur'ān selected for frequent recitation. The basis of their appeal must have been varied. As we have suggested above, dire threats of Judgment Day carry an explicit message to even the most unsophisticated hearer; indeed, it was in part by such warnings that the Prophet succeeded in making his earliest converts among the pagan Arabs. And the concept of a just retribution further signified, for Spanish Muslims, the hope of a divinely-ordained punishment against the Christians who had robbed them of their Islamic state and hence of their freedom; they might well yearn for a righting of that wrong in the world to come. Whatever the reason for their feelings, there is no question that the Last Judgment, as evoked in the Qur'ān, was a theme very close to their hearts.

The Manuscripts.

The material on which the present edition is based has been deliberately limited in breadth —to one short chapter of the Qur'ān, as explained above— and also in depth, to six MSS that contain the chapter in question. The criteria for selection of these particular MSS are, admittedly, arbitrary, and founded on practical considerations. Were it possible for an individual to examine all the extant Aljamiado versions of Sūra 79 (or of any other portion of the Qur'ān), he could determine from the beginning which MS would serve as the ideal base, and his presentation of the texts might differ considerably from ours. But in view of the fact that the MSS are so many and so widely scattered, and that any edition which aspired to include them all would reach colossal proportions, we have chosen to make a beginning using the few texts immediately available, planning to build subsequently upon this foundation. For these same reasons, no single MS has been chosen as the base text; rather, complete readings from all six are given. Our sample of material is too small to permit certain kinds of assumptions about the MS tradition. The edition of this one chapter of the Aljamiado Qur'ān is, therefore, not to be thought of as definitive, but rather as a contribution toward an eventual complete, critical text.

The six MSS are: two from the Biblioteca Nacional (National Library), Madrid: two from the Escuela de Estudios Arabes (School of Arabic Studies), Madrid; one from the Biblioteca Pública Provincial (Public Provincial Library), Toledo; and one from the Bibliothèque Nationale (National Library), Paris. Descriptions of all six follow (see also the photographic reproductions after p. 97).

Number 5078 of the Biblioteca Nacional, Madrid (hereafter BN 5078) is described in that library's catalogue of Arabic MSS [11]:

> CLXXIV. ALCORAN ABREVIADO.
>
> 4.º: papel.
> 35 fol.: ár. y aljamía: falto al principio y fin; maltratadísimo.
> Contiene un fragmento de una traducción y explicación de los textos alcoránicos en las Suras y aleyas I, 1; LXVII, 1; LXXVIII, 39; LXXIX, 41; LXXXI, 22; LXXXIV, 9; LXXXIX, 10 a 26; CI, 4; CIV, 1 [12].
>
> Comprende además:
> 2. Receta para las almorranas ...
> 3. Fragmento de una cuenta de sueldos ...
> 4. Fragmentos varios en ár. ...

The MS is also registered in Saavedra's index [13]. Sūra 79 occupies folios 24r 10 to 26v 15, at which point the text breaks off: folio 27r begins with Sūra 81 in the middle of verse 20. About two leaves must therefore have been lost before the text was numbered. In BN 5078, the Arabic text and its Aljamiado translation and commentary are written in alternating paragraphs.

The present number 425 of the Bibliothèque Nationale in Paris (henceforth P 425) was first described by Silvestre de Sacy in the Napoleonic period [14]. He noted that the MS was in very poor condition, lacking a beginning and end. Its surviving 116 leaves (plus 3 loose sheets in the binding) contain Sūras 36, verse 26 to the end; 59, verse 18 to the end; 67; and 78 to 113, inclusive. There are two lacunae, one of two leaves which must have contained parts of Sūras 83 and 84, and the other of one leaf, with the last words of 85 and the beginning of 86.

The current official catalogue of the Bibliothèque Nationale[15] contains the following statement:

> 425. Extraits du Coran accompagnés d'une traduction espagnole, écrite en caractères arabes. ... Ce manuscrit offre un example de cette mauvaise écriture maure-espagnole dont on se servait à Grenade au XVIe siècle.
> Papier. 119 feuillets. Hauteur, 20 cm.; largueur, 13 cm. et demi. 12 lignes par page. (Ancien fonds 108, Colbert 365_2.)

An additional leaf inserted opposite the first folio reads: "Hic liber manuscriptus arabicus, cuius principium parieter et finis desiderantur continet varias sententias, ac textus ex Alcorano deceptos cum interpretationes hispanica singulis subiecta caractere tamen mauritanico." And, below, "Sententia varia et lectiones ex Alcorano caractere Mauritanio, cum earundem expositione infra singulis subiecta; sed lingua veteri Hispanica caractere etiam Mauritanio". Sūra 79 occupies folios 45v 8 to 51r 7. Arabic and Aljamiado passages alternate; in the former the vowels are written in red, in the latter in black.

Number 39 of the Escuela de Estudios Arabes in Madrid (henceforth J 39) appears in that institution's catalogue as follows[16]:

> P.: Hilo flojo.—E.: Siglo XVI; sin fecha.—Let.: Magrebí.—Tin.: Negra. En los folios 1 a 32 hay epígrafes y vocales en tinta roja.—Tam.: 0,16 × 0,11 y 0,13.—C.: Oscila entre 0,11 × 0,18 y 0,12 × 0,07.—Lin.: Oscilan entre 14 y 7.—F.: 162.—En.: Cuadernos sueltos.—Pro.: Almonacid.—Len.: Arabe y aljamiada.

The unbound sheets that make up the volume contain, in addition to chapters from the Qur'ān, portions of *Kitāb ash-Shahāb* by Abū ᶜAbd Allah Muḥammad ibn Salm al-Qaḍāᶜī, and also of a collection of *ḥadīth*. Sūra 79 occupies folios 98r 1 to 102v 1, but its first five verses are missing: the text jumps from Sūra 9:128 at the bottom of folio 97v to the last words of 79:5 at the top of 98r. Since the volume is unbound, it was easy for leaves to be shuffled before the pages were numbered; some of the missing material, from Sūras 36, 67, 74, and 78, appears out of sequence later in the text[17]. Arabic and Aljamiado sections alternate.

The second MS from the Escuela de Estudios Arabes, J 25, is also summarized in the Ribera-Asín catalogue:

> P.: Hilo, grueso.—E.: Siglo XVI. Sin fecha.—Let.: Magrebí, clara; tinta negra con vocales rojas y epígrafes amarillos hasta el folio 85; en los demás, epígrafes rojos.—F.: 184 y 2 de guardas.—Tam.: 0,20 × 0,13.—C.: 0,15 × 0,09.—Lin.: 14.—En.: En piel de la época; restaurada.—Pro.: Almonacid.—Len.: Arabe y aljamiada.

The Qur'ānic passages (fragments of Sūras 1, 2, 3, 36, and 67, and all of 78-114) occupy the first hundred folios of the volume; Sūra 79 appears from 37r 5 to 41r 1. Other works contained in the same binding include (again to quote from the catalogue) *Aljotba de la Pascua de los adahaes; Aljotba para laljomúa que xe nonbra en ella la muerte y el día del judiçio; Aljotba de la Paxcua de Ramadán; Pedricaçión de la noche del leilato el cadri* ("narrada en forma casi exactamente igual que en el Evangelio de San Lucas, capítulo XV"). In this MS the Arabic Sūras of the Qur'ān were written first in widely-spaced lines, and the interlinear Aljamiado translation added subsequently. Several folios, including those containing *Sūrat an-Nāziᶜāt*, were reproduced photographically in P. Gil *et al.'s Colección de textos aljamiados*[18]. And as mentioned above (p. 15) the entire contents have been transliterated and published by J. Vernet and M. L. Moraleda.

Of the two descriptions of number 4938 of the Biblioteca Nacional (hereafter BN 4938), Guillén Robles' is the fuller:

> LXVII. ALCORAN. 4.º: papel: 15-50 cm. por 9-50: 14 lín pág.
> Falto al principio y fin.
> 65 fol.: magrebí: ár. y aljamía: el ár. en letra más gruesa que lo aljamiado: vocales en negro en éste, y en carmín en aquél: al principio, en una papeleta, una nota de Yriarte sobre el ms.: al principio de varias Suras, encabezamientos en color: las aleyas, separadas por adornos en carmín: maltratadísimo antes: restaurado hoy: encuad. imitación or., de Grimaud ...

Saavedra adds: "Letra clara, papel fuerte, de fines del siglo XV" [19]; we will discuss the validity of this date in the next section. The MS contains only Qur'ān [20], except that several pages of Arabic prayers with their Aljamiado translation have been inserted near the beginning and are numbered as folios 13r to 17v. Sūra 79 is found at 21r 6 to 24v 15. Arabic and Aljamiado passages alternate throughout. The MS has been fully edited as part of an unpublished doctoral dissertation [21], and some of its forms analyzed in a paper presented before the international Aljamiado congress [22].

MS number 235 of Toledo's Biblioteca Pública Provincial (henceforth T 235) is unique within this group of texts in several respects. It is the only one that bears a date (1606); the only one to contain a complete translation of the entire Qur'ān; the only one written in Latin script; the only one that consists entirely of translation and commentary, and includes none of the original Arabic text of the Qur'ān. The library's card catalogue describes it thus:

> [Alcorán]
> Fol. 1 vto. s. n. E. [Indice] Principio-l elaçora dellalhamdu lillehi. aleas i fo.
> Fol. 3 s. n. A: 114 elaçora de las fentes [*sic*]. 347 fo.
> Fol. 3 s. n. vto. E: 1 Alhandu lileehi es el principio del alcoran y es siete aleas. En el nombre de Alha [*sic*] piadoso de piedad. Fol. 347 vto. A: ... de los alchimes y de las gentes (sigue una inscripción árabe formularia).
>
> 1 g. + 4 h. bl. + 3 fol. s. n. + 347 fols. + 3 h. + 1 g. - 230 × 170 mm. C. esc. 160 × 100.—L. de principios del s. XVII. Texto en caracteres latinos escritos en negro. Títulos y pasajes, destacados en rojo hasta el fol. 105. Algunos sellos de la Bca. Nacional, donde figuró con el número 19473 - Cart.
>
> No figura en el estudio de González Palencia publicado en la Miscelánea de estudios y textos árabes.

Saavedra also includes the MS in his index [23], mentioning that it "contiene la traducción del Alcorán 'en letra de cristianos'". As the catalogue description states, certain passages in the first hundred folios stand out by being written in red ink. These are the interpolated selections of *tafsīr* or exegesis, which the scribe has been conscientious enough to distinguish from the words of the Qur'ān itself by the use of a different color. At folio 105 the scribe, apparently tired of switching pens, abandoned the red ink but continued to separate Qur'ānic from *tafsīr* material by setting off the latter between small diagonal slashes.

The translation of Sūra 79 is contained in folios 335v 13 to 336v 15. The first three lines, not reproduced in our comparative text, read: "el açora de annezi@ti es quarenta y quatro aleas + enel nombre de Allah piadoso de Piedad". The unusual marginal notes of T 235, written in Spanish, Arabic, and Aljamiado, are the subject of an article now in press [24].

Of the history and fortunes of these six MSS over the centuries, little or nothing is known. P 425 apparently formed part of a private collection (see the catalogue's reference to "Colbert") and had passed to the Bibliothèque Nationale by the end of the eighteenth century. J 39 and J 25 both were among the scores of Morisco MSS unearthed at Almonacid de la Sierra; they must have lain undisturbed in that hiding place at least since 1609. BN 4938 came to the Biblioteca Nacional from the private library of Pascual de Gayangos, but that energetic collector of Arabic and Aljamiado MSS left no information concerning its source. It was Gayangos, too, who informed Saavedra of the presence of T 235 in Toledo's public library, but as to how long it had been there, when it was moved there from the Biblioteca Nacional, and from whence it came before that, we remain in ignorance. Many Morisco MSS written in Latin, as opposed to Arabic, characters date from the period after the expulsion, and are to be found in the libraries of Tunisia and Morocco; but we have no particular reason to believe that this one was ever outside of Spain. The scribe, though punctilious about dating his text (his notations state that he finished copying the four quarters of the Qur'ān on May 2nd, May 31st, June 22nd [Thursday], and July 11th [Tuesday], respectively, in the year 1606), unfortunately does not inform us of his location or place of origin.

In taking up the six MSS in this order, the same order in which they are printed in the "Texts" section —BN 5078, P 425, J 39, J 25, BN 4938, and T 235— our criterion has not been chronological (for their chronology, see below under "Language"), but rather is based on the degree of the MSS's genetic relationship to each other, insofar as it can be determined. It is now necessary to justify such ordering. A comparison of the readings of the various MSS is the clue to deciding which of them represent merely different copies of a single translation, and which constitute entirely independent versions.

It is obvious at first glance that T 235 stands in a class by itself, and that the Qur'ān translation it contains, though dated as late as 1606, was not copied from any of the (presumably earlier) versions presented here. Proofs of its unique character include the readings of verses 2 through 5, where it alone renders the Arabic active participles literally (*arrancantes, andantes,* etc.); verses 20 and 34, where it dispenses entirely with the commentaries accumulated by the other texts; and the many verses in which its wording stands in contrast to that of all the other five MSS. See, for example, verse 17, with T 235's *desconoçe* vs. *a deškreido* elsewhere; 22, *volbio las cuestas* vs. *tornoše/bolbyoše rridra saga;* 27, *y su fraguaçion* vs. *ke lo frag(w)ó*; 29, *su sol y rresplandor* vs. *la klaredat del šol;* 31, *pastos* vs. *yerbaš;* 33, *animales* vs. *ganadoš;* 40, *apetitos* vs. *boluntad;* and many other instances. In our edition of the six MSS, T 235 has been placed last to emphasize its individuality.

In the remaining versions, similarities in wording are, for the most part, more noticeable than differences, so that the task of separating the text into families becomes a more delicate one. Yet a case may still be made for classifying BN 4938 apart from the rest. One of the features of this MS is its prolixity: the proportion of interpolated commentary to actual Qur'ānic text is unusually high. The most dramatic instance of this tendency is verse 20, in which the proportion of commentary to text is precisely ten words to one; but in many other verses as well, BN 4938 expands the other Aljamiado versions by at least a word or a phrase. Note, e. g., verse 1, with *še ponen i še funden* vs. *še funden* elsewhere; 2, *i ešmenoran loš gwešoš* added; 5, *i ordena lo ke le plaze* added; 8, *de myedo de Allah* added; 10, *para el konto* added, and so forth. It might be argued that what we have here is in fact a version originally akin to the others to which a later copyist added additional material; yet there are enough instances of markedly variant wording to make that argument doubtful. See verse 6, *el kwerno de Isrāfīl* vs. *la bozina* in the other five Aljamiado texts; 15, *ate plegado* vs. *ya te bino;* 16, *aši še kl[am]a* vs. *aši era šu nombre;* 19, *a la obidensya* vs. *al addīn;* 41, *ašentamyento* vs. *šošyego;* 46, *mannanada* vs. *mannana.* On the basis of all this evidence, then, we consider BN 4938 to be a separate translation of the Qur'ān, whose author may nonetheless have been familiar with the wording of other, more "standard" versions. That some kind of standard translation did exist, and was frequently copied, becomes clear after a comparison of the four remaining MSS.

Of the other four texts, two are unfortunately incomplete: J 39 lacks verses 1-5, and BN 5078 lacks 41-46. But the 35 verses which all four MSS do share show a high degree of affinity in their wording, undeniably too high to be the result of mere coincidence. Somewhere in the background of these MSS must be a single translation of the Qur'ān into Spanish or Aljamiado, annotated with selected passages of *tafsīr.* Such a text, with the appropriate commentary already, as it were, "made to order", would have circulated among the Moriscos of different parts of Spain over a considerable period of time; for, as our detailed study of the texts' language will show, MSS containing essentially the same wording nonetheless exhibit variations of phonology and morphology that can only be ascribed to differing times and places of origin.

A closer examination of the readings of the four MSS at issue bears out this claim. First, if we compare BN 5078 with P 425, it becomes clear that the two must be copied, if not from the very same MS, then from two MS versions of a single text. Readings which these two alone share include: in verse 7, *apreš d-ella šera la šegunda;* 9, *de akelloš šeran umileš enklinadoš;* 10, *tornadoš ḫaleqadoš nwebament(e)*; 14, *lwego šeran šobre la kara de la tyerra;* 19, *aw/abe myedo;* 25, *konprišolo Allah;* 27, *šinše pilareš;* 29, *nwey(te).* Either P 425 or its immediate predecessor, however, is obviously the work of a careless or unintelligent scribe, for he has on several occasions omitted or misunderstood portions of his original text. See the omission of *i el (la?) otro* at verse 7; of *i loš welloš* (or *oğoš*) at 9; and of *de šu nombramyento* at 43. Egregious errors of interpretation are *la follamyenta* for *afollamyento* at verse 22; *kyeren* for *kyere* or *kreyerá* at 38; and *prometimyento* for *porparamyento,* at 40. Neither the omissions nor these major errors have been corrected in our edition, even though the proper form is evident. Once again, until all MSS become available and make it feasible to prepare a truly critical text, it is more illuminating to present our few MSS substantially as they are written. We have emended, however, the abundant minor slips of P 425 such as omissions of single letters or of one-syllable words.

Though BN 5078 and P 425 are copies of essentially the same text, certain differences in their language show that P 425 is the more recent of the two. The Paris MS consistently restores final *-e,* which BN 5078 as consistently loses: verse 1, *šallyente* vs. *šallyent;* 13, *berdaderamente* vs. *berdaderament,* etc.; shows more "Castilian" treatment of diphthongs in *bašilloš, kwento* (3, 35) as against *bašyelloš* and *konto;* favors the numeral *kwarenta* over *kwaranta* (7), etc. These features may, of course , have originated in the MS that P 425 was copied from, rather than in P 425 itself, but in either case they contrast with BN 5078's greater archaism.

The precise nature of the two J MSS's relationship with the two above and with each other is the most difficult of all to determine. Of the 35 verses shared by the four texts, in seven the readings of all the MSS are virtually identical (verses 8, 17, 19, 23, 29, 32, 40). In an additional eleven verses, BN 5078, P 425, and J 39 are almost exactly the same, and J 25 differs only in omitting some phrase of commentary (verses 6, 7, 16, 20, 21, 26, 30, 33, 34, 36, 38), while in four instances, one MS or another differs from the other three only in supplying an additional word or phrase (verses 11, 15, 24, 25). Thus we have a total of twenty-two out of thirty-five verses, or nearly 63 %, in which these four MSS contain essentially the same wording, give or take a phrase added or omitted.

Within the group, the two J MSS clearly have a close relationship to one another: in verses 7, 9, 14, 19, 29, 35, and 37 they share readings which differ from those of BN 5078 and P 425. Yet at the same time, J 39 often differs from J 25 and joins the Madrid and Paris MSS (verses 12, 18, 20, 22, 26, 28, 30); in a very few instances the opposite occurs, and J 39 is excluded while the other three agree (verses 13, 25, 27, 33). It is this shifting panorama of relationships which complicates the search for the history of the four texts; yet it is undeniable that their common features far outweigh their differences, and that all of them reflect to some degree a widely-accepted Spanish version of the Qur'ān. BN 5078 and P 425, as we have shown, are copies of a single text, and the ancestor of J 39 probably had a great deal in common with that same text. J 25, with its greater compactness and shunning of commentary, stands somewhat apart, though its version might simply be the product of a "purist" scribe who excised from his copy what he considered to be extraneous material in the original.

Although we have affirmed above that BN 4938 contains an independent translation of the Qur'ān, it must be acknowledged that it, too, coincides at many points with the four MSS just discussed. At verses 32 and 36 its reading is identical to that of the others, and in several passages it differs from them only in adding an extra word or phrase: verses 10, 12, 13, 16, 17, 21, 22, 24, 26, 27, 29, 30, 31, 33, 34, 35, 38, 40 (eighteen out of thirty-five, or over 50 % of the verses that all five MSS share). This considerable similarity must be weighed against the instances already discussed in which BN 4938 departs sharply from the rest in its choice of words or expressions.

If, indeed, there circulated among the Moriscos some generally accepted translation of the Qur'ān into Aljamiado (as the close similarities among at least four of our MSS suggest), it is possible that that standard text might have descended from ᶜĪsā ibn Jābir's version of 1456. We know that ᶜĪsā's lost translation included not only the words of the Qur'ān itself, but selected commentaries on the text translated from the best Islamic authorities; and all the MSS which seem to follow a common standard incorporate just such exegetical passages. (The significant exception is T 235, whose wording confirms it as an independent translation.) It seems safe to conjecture that ᶜĪsā's Spanish Qur'ān of 1456, by virtue of its author's prestige, its completeness, and the usefulness of its interpolated commentaries, came to enjoy a wide circulation among the Moriscos in the next century and a half and to be copied repeatedly. Since it would not have been technically canonical nor imposed by any central authority, individual copyists could have taken some liberties in altering, abridging, or adapting it; at the same time, any Muslim with the skill and inspiration to translate the Qur'ān anew, on his own, would be free to do so. But the Moriscos' level of culture being what it was, by far the more common solution would be to reproduce the standard text. Four, perhaps five, of our copyists appear to have done just that; and when all the extant MSS are available in print and have been collated with each other, it will probably become evident that the majority of Aljamiado Qur'ān translations follow an established text, of which the most likely forefather is the Spanish version of ᶜĪsā ibn Jābir.

It may never be possible to trace the full history of the Aljamiado Qur'ān in manuscript. We know virtually nothing about the scribes —how they worked, where they obtained the texts they copied, how much contact they maintained with each other. The MSS that survive to the present day probably represent only a small percentage of the original number. And perhaps most fundamental of all, we have little information on Qur'ānic education or the tradition of Qur'ān recital among the Moriscos. Today, of course, if every written or printed Qur'ān were to disappear from the earth, the text could be reproduced instantly out of the memories of hundreds of thousands of Muslim *ḥāfiẓūn* (memorizers of the Qur'ān). Presumably some Moriscos likewise memorized their Scripture; but, especially late in the sixteenth century when their knowledge of its language had declined so much, did they learn it in Arabic? Or did they memorize simply the cut-down Spanish versions, interlarded with explanatory material, which these Aljamiado MSS reflect? If the scribes worked from memory even in part, that fact might explain the "overlapping" character of the texts at issue, several of which are clearly associated to some degree without showing signs of an actual genetic relationship. But this sample of six MSS, as we have asserted before, is too small to permit drawing any firm conclusions, much less to attempt reconstructing a stemma. What is certain is only the following: more than one translation of the Qur'ān into Spanish (or Aljamiado) existed. Within our group of texts, T 235 contains one independent version, while BN 5078 and P 425, both copies of a second, represent what we consider the "standard" translation. J 39 and J 25 are, respectively, somewhat more closely and somewhat more distantly related to that standard. BN 4938 combines strong reminiscences of the latter with a notable originality and independence of expression. It might be the product of a scribe who had memorized a standard version and reproduced it with variations, or of one with sufficient confidence to elaborate freely on his original. Or, the text could actually constitute and independent third translation of the Qur'ān, by a translator so thoroughly steeped in the accepted religious teaching of *tafsīr* that he arrived by coincidence at some of the same phrasing contained in other versions. Confirmation or rejection of these suggestions will have to await the publication of the other MSS of the Aljamiado Qur'ān.

Notes.

1 For a full account of the MS see C. López-Morillas, "Trilingual Marginal Notes (Arabic, Aljamiado, and Spanish) in a Morisco Manuscript from Toledo", forthcoming in *JAOS*.

2 "Juan de Segovia y el primer Alcorán trilingüe", *And*, XIV (1949), 149-173; and *Juan de Segovia y el problema islámico* (Madrid, 1952).

3 Classic works on the history of the Spanish Moriscos include: P. Boronat y Barrachina, *Los moriscos españoles y su expulsión* (Valencia, 1857); H. C. Lea, *The Moriscos of Spain* (Philadelphia, 1901; repr. New York, 1968); and P. Longás, *Vida religiosa de los moriscos* (Madrid, 1915). For a recent comprehensive treatment and up-to-date bibliography see A. Domínguez Ortiz and B. Vincent, *Historia de los moriscos: vida y tragedia de una minoría* (Madrid, 1978).

4 The most dramatic discovery of such a cache was that at Almonacid de la Sierra, Aragon, in 1884. Most of these MSS found their way to the Junta para la Ampliación de Estudios and are catalogued by J. Ribera and M. Asín, *Manuscritos árabes y aljamiados de la Biblioteca de la Junta* (Madrid, 1912). Other catalogues of the principal MS collections which contain Morisco Qur'āns are: H. Derenbourg, *Les manuscrits arabes de l'Escurial*

(Paris, 1884); F. Guillén Robles, *Catálogo de los manuscritos árabes existentes en la Biblioteca Nacional de Madrid* (Madrid, 1889); G. Levi della Vida, "Manoscritti arabi di origine spagnole nella Biblioteca Vaticana", *Collectanea Vaticana in honorem Anselmi M. Card. Albareda,* II (Rome, 1962), 181-184; E. Saavedra, "Indice general de la literatura aljamiada", Appendix to *Discurso leído ante la Real Academia Española* (Madrid, 1878), repr. in *Memorias de la Real Academia Española,* VI (1889), 140-328; and E. Terés Sádaba, *Los manuscritos árabes de la Real Academia de la Historia. La "Colección Gayangos"* (Madrid, 1975).

5 Sūra 81 : 1-2.

6 E. g., from Sūra 79 alone: *baša* for *beš,* 79 : 7; *ridrasara* for *rridra saga,* 79 : 22; *afugo* for *afogo,* 79 : 25; *šin šebilareš* for *šinše pilareš,* 79 : 28; *miyendo* for *miyedo,* 79 : 40; *les paresera* for *no leš paresera,* 79 : 46.

7 Two earlier studies touch on Morisco versions of the Qur'ān: E. Teza, "Di un compendio del Corano in espagnolo con lettere arabiche (manoscritto fiorentino)", *Rendiconti della Reale Accademia dei Lincei. Cl. di scienze morale, storiche e filologiche,* Series 4, no. 7 (1891), 81-88; and K. V. Zetterstéen, "Some Chapters of the Koran in Spanish Transliteration", *MO,* V (1911), 39-41. Other works of some relevance to the present study include: M.-T. d'Alverny, "Deux traductions latines du Coran au Moyen Age", *Archives d'histoire doctrinale et littéraire du Moyen Age,* XXIII (1948), 69-131; M. M. Moreno, "È lecito ai musulmani tradurre il Corano?", *OM,* V (1925), 532-543; D. Rahbar, "Aspects of the Qur'ān Translation", *Babel,* IX (1963), 60-68; A. L. Tibawi, "Is the Qur'ān Translatable? Early Muslim Opinion", *MW,* LII (1962), 4-16; and S. M. Zwemer, "Translations of the Koran", *MW,* V (1915), 244-261.

8 L. P. Harvey, *The Literary Culture of the Moriscos 1492-1609. A Study Based on the Extant Manuscripts in Arabic and Aljamía,* unpublished D. Phil. dissertation (Magdalen College, Oxford, 1958), 270.

9 J. Vernet has compared passages from two MSS, J 25 and J 18, and finds that they contain different translations (*BRABLB,* XXXV [1973-74], 188-189); but two texts are too small a sample on which to base general conclusions.

10 R. Menéndez Pidal, "Poema de Yúçuf. Materiales para su estudio", *RABM,* VII : 2 (1902), 91-129, 276-309, 347-362. Reprinted in the Colección Filológica de la Universidad de Granada, I (Granada, 1952).

11 By Guillén Robles; see n. 4, above.

12 This numbering of the passages is inaccurate. BN 5078 in fact contains Sūras 1 : 7; 2 : 1-3, 163, 207, 255-256, 284, 286; 3 : 1-6, 18-19, 26-27; 9 : 128-129; 26 : 78-79; 28 : 88; 30 : 17-19; 33 : 40-44; 36 : 1-83; 59 : 18-24; 67 : 1-2; 78 : 27-40; 79 : 1-41; 81 : 22-29; 82 : 1-19; 83 : 1-36; 84 : 1-9; 89 : 11-20; 101 : 4-11; 102 : 1-8; 103 : 1-3; 104 : 1-2.

13 As number XLVI, p. 271.

14 A. I. Silvestre de Sacy, *Notices et extraits des manuscrits de la Bibliothèque Nationale,* IV (Paris, An 7), 626-647.

15 W. MacGuckin de Slane, *Catalogue des manuscrits arabes de la Bibliothèque Nationale,* IV-1-B (Paris, 1883), 124.

16 By Ribera and Asín: see n. 4, above.

17 The entire contents of J 39 are Sūras 1 : 1-7; 2 : 1-5, 163, 255-257, 284-286; 3 : 1-6, 18-19, 26-27; 9 : 128; 36 : 68-83; 67 : 1-30; 74 : 54-55; 78 : 1-38; 79 : 6-46; 80 : 1-9, 13-42; 81 : 1-14; 87 : 16-19; 88 : 1-26; 89 : 1-30; 90 : 1-7; 91 : 14-15; and 92-114, complete.

18 P. Gil, J. Ribera, and M. Sánchez, *Colección de textos aljamiados* (Zaragoza, 1888), 153-163.

19 No. XXII, p. 255.

20 Sūras 3 : 1-4, 27; 9 : 128-129; 12 : 101; 26 : 78-89; 59 : 22-24; 67 : 1-30; 78 : 14-40; 79 : 1-46; 80 : 1-42; 81 : 1-8, 10-29; 82-100, complete; 101 : 1-7, 9-11; 102-105, complete.

21 C. López-Morillas, *Lexical and Etymological Studies in the Aljamiado Koran (Manuscript 4938 of the Biblioteca Nacional, Madrid)* (University of California, Berkeley, 1974).

22 C. López-Morillas, "Etimologías escogidas del Corán aljamiado (Manuscrito 4938 de la Biblioteca Nacional de Madrid)", *Actas,* 365-371.

23 No. LVI, p. 277.

24 See n. 1, above.

II. Language of the texts.

The system of transliteration of Aljamiado texts has evolved gradually toward a common standard in the course of the last century. The earliest transcriptions were designed chiefly to make the texts readily comprehensible *as Spanish* to a Spanish readership, and therefore adopted the orthographic conventions of that language: *j* for [x], *x* for [š], *c* for [k], and so on. Vowels in Arabic words were treated somewhat cavalierly (e. g., *aljotba* for *al-khuṭba, leilato* for *lailatu*), and Arabic emphatic and pharyngeal consonants were given no special representation at all[1].

In this century, a far more accurate system of transliteration was perfected by A. R. Nykl in his edition of the *Rrekontami*^{y}*ento del rrey Ališand*^{e}*re*[2]. In the very title of the work we can see one of the system's basic characteristics, the placing of "superfluous" vowels and consonants above the line of print. The syllabic structure of Classical Arabic requires that every syllable-initial consonant be followed by a vowel (i. e., it does not permit syllable-initial consonant clusters). Hence Morisco scribes, in slavish imitation of Arabic practice, broke up initial Spanish clusters by inserting a homorganic vowel: *entarar, pirimero, porometer, Ališandere.* The glides /w/ and /y/ which are the first elements of Spanish rising diphthongs are, when they follow a consonant, likewise preceded by a vowel: *puweš, siyelo, rrekontamiyento.* These extra vowels were unquestionably mere orthographic conventions, and not pronounced; but it has become the practice to reproduce them in transliteration, either above the line as in Nykl's edition or between parentheses, e. g. *ent(a)rar.*

The present edition dispenses with that convention, as well as altering certain other elements of traditional Aljamiado transcription. As a recent penetrating book review has pointed out[3], many features of the standard transliteration are not only distracting and hard on the eyes, but linguistically inaccurate as well. Editors are still clinging too closely to Spanish orthography: for instance, since the diphthong /we/ is spelled in Spanish *ue,* it is the *w* in the Aljamiado sequence *uwe* which has been treated as superfluous, hence the spellings *pu*^{w}*eš* or *pu(w)eš*; phonetically, of course, the *w*-glide is the indispensable element. Here we render the rising diphthongs as *we* and *ye,* respectively. Similarly, Aljamiado نّ , where it stands for the Spanish palatal nasal, has conventionally been transcribed as *ñ* in obedience to Spanish spelling; we give it as *nn,* not only more accurate but a neater match for the transcription of the palatal lateral as *ll.*

It may seem unfortunate to offer a new system of transliteration now, when an increasing number of Aljamiado texts are being published in the standard system, the only one sanctioned by the ongoing Colección de Literatura Española Aljamiado-Morisca[4]. But the greater accuracy and readability of the present texts may convince other *aljamiadistas* of the value of the change.

The following is a list of correspondences between the Arabic letters of the MSS and the Latin ones of our transliteration (for the sake of completeness we include the entire Arabic alphabet, although not all of its letters occur in these texts).

Consonants:

ا (*alif*, with or without *hamza*): not transliterated in Spanish words, where it serves chiefly to separate two vowels in hiatus (e. g., شَاَآمُشْ = *šeamoš*). In Arabic words, ' (apostrophe).

ب (*bā'*): *b*.

بّ : *p* in Spanish words, *bb* in Arabic ones.

ت (*tā'*): *t*.

ث (*thā'*): *ṯ*.

ج (*jīm*): *ğ*.

جّ : *č* in Spanish words, *ğğ* in Arabic ones.

ح (*ḥā'*): *ḥ*.

خ (*khā'*): *ḫ*.

د (*dāl*): *d*.

ذ (*dhāl*): *d*. Morisco scribes often used *dhāl* to render the fricative allophone of *d* which occurs between vowels, e. g., أَمَذُ = *amado*; standard transcription reproduces this practice faithfully by use of *đ* or *ḏ*. But an examination of our texts shows such inconsistency in the distribution of *dāl* and *dhāl* as to make it meaningless to distinguish between them in transliteration.

ر (*rā'*): *r*.

رّ : *rr*.

ز (*zāy*): *z*.

س (*sīn*): *s*.

ش (*shīn*): *š*.

شّ : *šš*[5].

ص (*ṣād*): *ṣ*.

ض (*ḍād*): *ḍ*.

ط (*ṭā'*): *ṭ*.

ظ (*ẓā'*): *ẓ*.

ع (*ᶜayn*): *ᶜ*.

غ (*ghayn*): *g*.

ف (*fā'*): *f*.

ق (*qāf*): *q*. Note that in the MSS *fā'* and *qāf* appear in their Maghribī form, ڢ and ڧ, respectively.

ك (*kāf*): *k*.

ل (*lām*): *l*.

لّ : *ll*.

م (*mīm*): *m*.

ن (*nūn*): *n*.

نّ : *nn*.

ه (*hā'*): *h*.

و (*wāw*): *w*.

ي (*yā'*): *y*.

Vowels:

َ (*fatḥa*): *a*.

َا (*fatḥa* plus *alif*): *e* in Spanish words, *ā* in Arabic ones.

ِ (*kasra*): *i*; if followed by *yā'*, *ī*.

ُ (*ḍamma*): *o* or *u* in Spanish words, according to their etyma, *u* whenever there is doubt (as in *sobir* vs. *subir*); *u* in Arabic words. If followed by *wāw*, *ō* or *ū* in Spanish, *ū* in Arabic.

Additional points:

The superfluous vowel added by the scribes to consonant clusters has been suppressed: اَنْتَرَر = *entrar*. It may be assumed that the vowel was identical with the following one; any exceptions, e. g. تِنْبَلَنْتَاشْ = *tinblanteš* (lit. *tinbelanteš*) are mentioned in footnotes.

The sequences *uwe* and *iye* after a consonant are rendered as *we, ye,* as stated above. The sequence *iy* before a vowel may represent either a vocalic or a consonantal sound, and the two cases have been transcribed differently: غِيُ = *gío* 'I guide', vs. غِيُ = *gyó* 'he guided'. Where *iy* stands for the conjunction 'and' before a word beginning with a vowel, it appears as *y*-: اِيَا نْتَا رَا = *y-entre*; before a consonant, as *i*.

A few observations on the orthography of T 235, the sole MS written in Roman letters. *B* and *v* are completely confused: *bal 16, volbio 22, estubieron 46* (*vozina 6, 13* [< BŪCINA], like modern Spanish *bocina,* shows the influence of VŌCE 'voice'). Anti-etymological *h* appears in *huesos 11*; the consonant in *humilladas 9, comprehendiolo 25,* and *habemos 10* merely reflects Latin orthography, but cf. *abrá 8, 35.*

Confusion of the voiceless and voiced sibilants may be seen in *corazones 8, deçian 10,* and *alteça 28.* The MS employs *ç* before both front and back vowels: *desconoçe 17, çielo 27, alço 28*; *ç* renders an Arabic *s* in *Muçe 15.* Voiceless and voiced palatal sibilants are distinguished, *vaxillos 3, dixeron 12* vs. *rrige 5.* The initial voiced palatal affricate in a Romance word is *g* (*gente 23*), but Arabic *jīm* is rendered as *ch* (*chehannam 39, alchanna 41*), suggesting that it was perceived as voiceless when initial or post-consonantal. Single *-s-* represents the voiceless sibilant in *fuesas 10.*

Other orthographic features include: a special graphic symbol for *rr* (resembling a capital letter), used always when the sound is initial and occasionally when it is medial; *v* for the vowel in *vn 13, vna 46; qu* before *a* in *quando 11, 16.* Two abbreviations are employed, *q* for *que* (*2, 3,* etc.) and *vr̄o(s)* for *vuestro(s)* (*24,*

33). Use of upper- and lower case initials is inconsistent (though proper names always have lower case) and has been regularized in the edited text.

The six MSS of Sūra 79 which form the basis for this study differ from each other in their language; and while the differences may not always appear great, they are nonetheless significant. The texts span most of the sixteenth century, a period of linguistic change in the Iberian Peninsula, and moreover proceed from an area, the northeast, that was subject to all sorts of dialect pressures. The native Aragonese speech, phonologically more conservative than Castilian, had at this period been subjected to centuries of influence from the latter, which was politically and culturally in the ascendant. To the east lay Catalan and Gallo-Romance, two language groups exercising great cultural and political sway. Any group of texts composed in this fluid set of circumstances over a period of decades must inevitably show effects of the give-and-take among competing dialects, learned and popular traits, innovation and conservatism.

We have organized this section so as first to provide an impression of the language of the MSS as a whole: they constitute, after all, six versions of a single text. Thus, initially, the data from all the MSS are combined under each category of phonology, morphology, etc. Presented in this fashion they will seem heterogeneous and even, at times, contradictory: for instance, *nwey*(*te*) and *wellos̆* (with diphthongization before a palatal) as against *noc̆e* and *oğos̆* (showing no diphthongization) are the solutions of different MSS. Subsequently, following this overall description, we group the linguistic features of the various versions by individual MS, in order to establish the relative chronology of the texts. Here it will become clear, to repeat the same example, that the MS which consistently diphthongizes before *yod* can be considered earlier (because less subject to Castilian influence) than the one that does not. Because only one of the MSS is dated and none indicates its place of origin, such internal evidence is the only basis for determining the history of these examples of the Aljamiado Qur'ān.

References are to Qur'ān verse (in italic Arabic numerals) followed by a colon and the number of the MS(S) in which the feature occurs (in regular Arabic numerals): e. g., *27*: 5078, 4938. Only one or two citations are given in each case; for complete references, see the Glossary.

In order to increase the usefulness of this study to the interested reader, we have keyed every point in the description of the language to previous grammatical analyses of Aljamiado texts. These provide an immediately relevant body of literature into which the present material may be fitted, as well as a source of additional data for consultation. The texts so used for reference are the following:

P. Yúçuf: R. Menéndez Pidal, *Poema de Yúçuf: Materiales para su estudio* (Granada, 1952); "Lenguaje del poema", pp. 63-94.

R. Alis̆.: A. R. Nykl, "Aljamiado Literature. *El Rrekontami^{y}ento del Rrey Alis̆and^{e}re*", *Revue Hispanique,* LXXVII (1929), 409-611; "Language", pp. 448-465.

Alj. T.: R. Kontzi, *Aljamiadotexte. Ausgabe mit einer Einleitung zur Sprache und Glossar,* 2 vols. (Wiesbaden, 1974); "Aragonismen" and "Arabismen", I, pp. 49-162.

Batallas: A. Galmés de Fuentes, *El libro de las batallas: Narraciones épico-caballerescas,* 2 vols. (Madrid, 1975); "Estudio lingüístico", II, pp. 9-104.

Where a given feature is discussed in any of these works, the reader is referred to title and page number; in the absence of any such citation it may be assumed that the phenomenon is limited to the present group of texts.

Phonology.

Stressed vowels. Ŏ sometimes diphthongizes before a palatal, a phenomenon characteristic of Aragonese[6]: *nwey 29*: 5078, *nweyte 29*: 425, *wellos̆ 9*: 5078 (but cf. *noc̆e 29*: 39, 25, *oğos̆ 9, 20*: 4938) [*P. Yúçuf*, 65-66; *Alj. T.*, 52; *Batallas*, 34]. Ŏ > *wa*: *gwas̆os̆ 11*: 5078[7]. Ĕ, Ŏ diphthongize where the Castilian counterparts do not: *rryedra 22*: 5078, *fwes̆as̆ 10*: 5078, 39, 25, 4938 [*R. Alis̆.*, 455]. Ŏ fails to diphthongize: *konto 10, 12, 14*: 4938, *35*: 5078 (but cf. *kwento 35*: 425) [*R. Alis̆.*, 455]. There are no cases of diphthongization of *ę*, *ọ* [*P. Yúçuf*, 66; *R. Alis̆.*, 455; *Batallas*, 34]. *Yé* is reduced to *i* before a palatal in *bas̆illos̆ 3*: 25 (*vaxillos 3*: 235), vs. *bas̆yellos̆ 3*: 5078, 4938 [*Alj. T.*, 52]. The same reduction takes place without the presence of a palatal in *rridra 22*: 39, 25. *Wé* is monophthongized in *kulebra 22*: 5078, 39, vs. *kulwebra 22*: 4938. -ARIU generally becomes *-ero*, as in *sagero 34*: 39, 4938 (cf. patently learned *altaryo 28*: 4938).

Unstressed vowels, pretonic. Ē, Ĕ both may raise to *i*: *obidensya 4*: 25, 4938 (cf. *obedensya 4*: 5078), *mintros̆a 12*: 4938, *s̆obirano 24*: 5078, 4938 (cf. *s̆oberano 24*: 39, 25, 235), *s̆igirá 7*: 39, *tinblantes̆ 8*: 5078, 25 (cf. *tenblantes̆ 8*: 39) [*R. Alis̆.*, 455]. *Ins̆enplo 26*: 4938 could represent a prefix change. Ĭ > *e* (showing popular rather than learned transmission) in *klaredat 29*: 5078, 4938, *enklinados̆ 9*: 5078. A frequent vacillation in the pretonic vowels is that between *a* and *e*: *abantağara 38*: 4938, *abentajara 38*: 235; *mandamyento 18*: 5078, *mandemyento 18*: 25 [*Batallas*, 37]. (In *des̆konosyent 37*: 425 vs. *des̆konesyent 37*: 5078, two competing verb endings are involved.) Note the variants *es̆keresyo 29*: 425 and *es̆kurasyo 29*: 25 beside *es̆kuresyo 29*: 5078, 39. The intertonic vowel is preserved in *tremulantes̆ 8*: 4938, an Aragonese form[8] (cf. *tenblantes̆ 8*: 39) and *esbuludreando 8*: 235 (where the scribe, copying into Roman script, may inadvertently have imitated the "superfluous" vowel of his Aljamiado original.) Apheresis occurs in the single case *bantallará 38*: 5078.

Unstressed vowels, posttonic. Final *-e* falls frequently after *nt*: *berdaderament 13*: 5078, 4938, *nwebament 10*: 5078, 4938, *ğent 23, 26*: 5078 (but cf. *-mente 10, 13*: 425, *ğente 23*: 39, 25) [*P. Yúçuf*, 67; *R. Alis̆.*, 455; *Batallas*, 34-35]. It is lost after other consonants in *bal 16*: 5078, 39, 25, 4938, 235, *aw* (imperative of *aber*) *19*: 5078 (cf. *abe 19*: 425), and *nweb 20*: 5078 (beside *nwebe 20*: 425, 39). (In *es̆pleyte 33*: 25, 4938, 235 *-e* has been added to a word borrowed from Old Provençal, but cf. *es̆pleyt 33*: 5078). Final *-o* disappears only once, in *mintros̆ 12*: 39 [*P. Yúçuf*, 67-68; *R. Alis̆.*, 445; *Batallas*, 34-35]. The preposition *ad* (which in Aragonese retains its etymological consonant before a word beginning in a vowel, especially an *a*)[9] [*P. Yúçuf*, 85; *Batallas*, 61-63] acquires a redundant *-a* in the phrase *ada Allah 19*: 5078, 39, 25, 235.

Initial single consonants. F- is preserved in a majority of cases: always before *we* (*fwego 34*: 5078, 39, 4938, *fwerte 27*: 5078, 25, 4938, *fwes̆as̆ 10*: 5078, 39, 25, 4938, and in the perfect tense of *ser* and *ir*), elsewhere in *fizo 20*: 5078 (but cf. *hizo 20*: 4938), *funden 1*: 5078, 25, 4938, 235, *fuyendo 22*: 5078, 25, 4938, etc. [*P. Yúçuf*, 73; *R. Alis̆.*, 455-456; *Alj. T.*, 53-54; *Batallas*, 26-28]. *H-* (aspirate) is the norm in J 39; this MS preserves the aspirate in *hata 33* (< Ar. *ḥattā*), which BN 4938 offers in the hypercorrect form *fašta*. *Gwešoš 2*: 4938, *11*: 39, 25, 4938 shows velar reinforcement of the initial labial; in *gayata 22*: 4938 an initial C- is voiced.

Initial Clusters. Both PL- and CL- remain in some MSS, but are palatalized in others (see below, p. 44), *plegado 15*: 4938, *18*: 5078, 25 vs. *llegado 18*: 39; *klamó 16*: 5078, 25, 4938 vs. *llamó 16*: 39, 235 [*P. Yúçuf*, 72; *R. Ališ.*, 456; *Alj. T.*, 54-55; *Batallas*, 42-43]. (The texts contain no item with initial FL-.) *Kridó 24*: 25 fails to voice the initial stop, [*R. Ališ.*, 456] but cf. *gritó 24*: 235.

Medial single consonants. Though Aragonese tends to preserve voiceless stops, -T- here remains unvoiced only in *gayata 22*: 4938 [*P. Yúçuf*. 73-74; *R. Ališ.*, 456; *Batallas*, 44]. Voicing of -C- occurs regularly: *agwa 30*: 5078, 39, 4938, *fragwó 27*: 25, 4938; note the further erosion of the resulting *-g-* in *awa 31*: 5078 and *frawó 27*: 5078. Preservation of -D- is another Aragonese characteristic: here -D- usually remains only in the word *ǧudisyo 42*: 39, 25, 4938, but cf. *ǧwisyo 42*: 425 [*P. Yúçuf*, 71-72; *R. Ališ.*, 456; *Batallas*, 43-44]. In *preika*[*dor*] *45*: 39 a -D- has fallen (cf. semi-learned *pedrikador 45*: 425, 25, 4938), but it is unusual that the velar should fail to voice, as in OCast. *preigar*; either the word is still subject to some learned pressure, or the missing dental results from a scribal slip. In *rrebibkar 10*: 25, *rrebibkadoš 10*: 39 an original -F- (*RE-VĪVIFICĀRE) has become *b*, perhaps after earlier vocalization (**rebiwcar*); note that the *c* is preserved as voiceless.

Because of the peculiar nature of the Aljamiado script, which reflects the imposition of Arabic rules of syllable structure upon Spanish (see above, p. 27), it is not always possible to tell when a *-y-* is being used as an anti-hiatic device between vowels —that is, reflects an actual pronunciation— and when it is merely an orthographic sign. A few contrasts in spelling, such as *šeyer 10*: 5078, 4938 vs. *šer 10*: 25, 39, probably reflect the presence of a true (pronounced) *-y-* in the first case, since the two MSS in question have a more marked Aragonese flavor [10]. Similarly, the spelling *trayran 34*: 5078, 39, 4938 may indicate an underlying infinitive *trayer* [11], though here the *y* could result merely from the closing of *e* to a semivowel in hiatus (*traeran* > *trayran*). In other instances a *y* is clearly the orthographic representation of a semiconsonant, and our transliteration reflects the fact: *rryedra* for the MS's reading *rriyedera* (*22*: 5078). While we have generally been conservative in retaining the *y* in doubtful cases, one cannot hope to determine, on the basis of these or other Aljamiado texts, the true frequency of anti-hiatic *-y-* [*P. Yúçuf*, 67; *R. Ališ.*, 457; *Batallas*, 35-36]. (T 235, the only version using Roman script, contains *creyente 2*, *descreyente 10* and *mayor 20, 34*, as in Castilian. In *comprehendiolo 25* the *-h-* is presumably silent.)

Medial geminates and clusters. -FF- is simplified in *afogó 25*: 5078, 25, 4938, then aspirated in *ahogó 25*: 39. -CT- > [i̯t] in *nwey*(*te*) *29*: 5078, 425 and *feyto 44*: 425, but cf. *noče 29*: 39, 25, 4938, 235, and *hečo 44*: 39, the more common solutions [*P. Yúçuf*, 69-70; *R. Ališ.*, 456; *Alj. T.*, 55-56; *Batallas*, 49-50]. (*Ešpleyt*[*e*] *33*: 5078, 25, 4938, 235 is borrowed from OProv. *espleit* < EXPLICITU.) -LT- gives only *č*, *mučo 42*: 4938, *43*: 39. -C'L- yields both palatal *-ll-* (*welloš 9*: 5078) and fricative /ž/ (*ogoš 9, 20*: 4938) [*P. Yúçuf*, 70-71; *R. Ališ.*, 457; *Alj. T.*, 56-57; *Batallas*, 45-49]. The present participle *šallyent*(*e*) *1*: 425, 25, 39, 4938 reflects an infinitive *sallir*, with *-l-* palatalized by spread of the *yod* in SALIO [*Batallas*, 57]. (*A*)*bantallará 38*: 5078, 39, 25 is a hypercorrection: *abantağará 38*: 4938 with the fricative is borrowed from Fr. *avantage* via Prov., Cat.

avantatge. The -M'L- cluster is resolved in two ways: by learned preservation of the intervening vowel (*tremulanteš 8*: 4938), or by inserting a bilabial in the typical "Castilian" fashion (*šenblante 26*: 5078, 39; *tinblanteš 8*: 5078, 25; *rretiemblante 7*: 235).

Final consonants. Devoicing of *-d* to *-t* occurs in *klaredat 29*: 5078, 4938 and *boluntat 40*: 5078, but cf. *klaredad 29*: 39, 25 and *boluntad 40*: 39, 25, 4938 [*R. Ališ.*, 456; *Batallas*, 50]. Final *-t* is lost in *nwey 29*: 5078. The preposition *parad 45*: 25 shows preservation of the etymological *-d* of PER AD before following *a*, cf. *ada*. In *bal 16*: 5078, 425, 39 an *-ll* has been depalatized when left in final position through the loss of *-e*. And *aw 19*: 5078, imperative of *aber*, must be the result of an *abe* (as in *19*: 425) > **ab* in which the final consonant vocalized (cf. *nuu* < NUBE, *R. Ališ.*, 115v). The only instance of confusion of sibilants in one of the Aljamiado MSS (beside several in T 235, written in Latin script) occurs in final position: *beš 20*: 4938, for *bes* (noun).

Sporadic consonant changes. Dissimilation of nasals has taken place in *lonbramyento 43*: 4938, beside *nonbramyento 43*: 39, 25 and *nonbre 16*: 5078, 39 [*R. Ališ.*, 456]. Metathesis occurs in *eškrubirše 36*: 425. *Pedrikador 45*: 425, 25 is a metathesized variant of *preikador 45*: 39. *Miraglo 20*: 4938, the etymological form, contrasts with metathesized *milagro 20*: 5078, 39, 25, 235. *Prešona 35, 40*: 5078, 4938, as against *peršona 35, 40*: 425, 39, 25, 235, may be the result either of metathesis or of the confusion of two common prefixes [*P. Yúçuf*, 74; *R. Ališ.*, 457; *Batallas*, 50-51].

Elision and apocope. The *-e* of certain prepositions, pronouns, etc., is sometimes dropped before a following *e-*. Prepositions: *d-ella 7*: 5078, 39, 25, *dellos 7*: 235, *d-ešte 25*: 4938, 235; *šobr-el 30*: 5078 (before the masculine definite article). Conjunction *ke*: *k-el 6*: 4938 (before the definite article), *k-él 17*: 39, 25 (before the masculine subject pronoun). Interrogative pronoun *ke*: *ké-štaš 43*: 425, 39. Reflexive pronoun: *š-entyende 14, 42*: 4938, *š-era 20*: 4938. The *-e* is elided before an *a-* in *d-andadura 28*: 4938, *d-aber 45*: 4938, and *eškubrirš-a 36*: 4938. In *ke-l 35*: 5078, the *-e* of the indirect object pronoun *le* has been elided in enclitic position after the conjunction [*R. Ališ.*, 457-458].

Morphology and Syntax.

Noun. *Mar* appears generally as feminine (*3, 25*: 5078, 25, 4938), once as masculine (*3*: 235). *Fin* may also be of either gender (feminine *44*: 425, 39, 235, masculine *44*: 4938)[12]. In *kul(w)ebra 22*: 5078, 39, 4938 vs. *kulebro 22*: 425, 4938, as in *tornada 12*: 425, 25, 4938, 235 vs. *tornado 12*: 5078, 39, the difference in gender does not reflect any perceptible difference in meaning.

Article. Most nouns borrowed from Arabic have the Arabic article *al-* attached, and take a redundant Spanish definite article: *loš almalakeš 2*: 5078, 25, 4938, *el alǧanna(h) 41*: 39, 25. [*R. Ališ.*, 458; *Alj. T.*, 70]. (The phrase *al allannabī 42*: 4938 'to the Prophet' is doubly redundant.) The definite article, when occurring before an initial vowel in the next word, occasionally retains its etymological *ll*: *ell otro mundo 38*: 4938, *ell agwa 30*: 425, 39, 4938 [*P. Yúçuf*, 76; *R. Ališ.*, 458].

Use of the feminine article before *un* and/or a masculine noun or pronoun, *entre la un tokamyento i la otro 7*: 5078, *la otro 38*: 5078, finds a close parallel in Old Aragonese "la huno ..., el otro"[13].

Personal pronoun. *Lo, loš* is consistently the masculine direct object pronoun for both persons and things; *le, leš* is the indirect object form for persons, both masculine and feminine. Placement of the object pronouns in relation to the verb follows, in the great majority of cases (some 85 %), the norms of Old Spanish: when the verb is the first element of the breath group and is preceded by no secondary stress (conjunctions such as *i* do not take secondary stress), the pronoun is enclitic; when the verb is not the first stressed element in the breath group, the pronoun is proclitic [14]. Examples of the two cases from the text include: (enclitic) *¿Ate plegado ...? 15*: 4938; *I dišole Allah 17*: 4938; *I giyarte a 19*: 5078; (proclitic) *kwando lo klamó 16*: 25, *para ke le ayaš myedo 19*: 4938, *¡ke no le akaeska ...! 26*: 39. The modern rules for object-pronoun placement, by which pronouns are enclitic only after affirmative commands, infinitives, and gerunds, evolved in the course of the 16th century [15], and although our texts belong precisely to that period, it is not surprising that the general archaism of Aljamiado should keep them close to Old Spanish in this respect.

The Aragonese tendency to use the subject pronoun after prepositions [16] can be seen in the single instance *¿A tu es en que creas ...? 18*: 235 [*P. Yúçuf*, 76; *R. Ališ*, 459; *Alj. T.*, 59-61; *Batallas*, 52-53].

Relative pronoun. Forms are *ke 1, 2, 3, 4, 5*: 5078, 4938, etc. (very frequent); *kyen* both as subject (*37*: 5078, 425, 39, 25, 4938) and as object of a preposition (*26, 36*: 5078, 425, 39, 25, 4938); *lo ke* neuter as object of a preposition (*26*: 5078, 425, 39, 4938; *35*: 5078, 425, 39, 25, 4938); and *kwando* apparently used as a relative in *el rrekontamyento de Mūsā kwando lo klamó šu šennor 15-16*: 5078, 25, 4938.

Demonstrative pronoun. Only a limited number of forms occur: *ešte 20*: 5078, *ešto 42*: 4938, beside *akešte 25*: 5078, 425, 25; *akešta 25*: 39; and *akel 20*: 5078, 425, 39, *akella 12*: 25, 235, *akello* (neut.) *26, 30*: 425, 39, 25.

Possessive pronoun. Note how in *šu ǧenteš 23*: 4938 the *-š* of the possessive has been deleted before the initial palatal of the following noun. The Aragonese possessive *lur, lures* does not appear [*P. Yúçuf*, 78-79; *R. Ališ.*, 459].

Indefinite pronoun. Otro 38: 235; *šemeǧante, šenblante* (*de*) 'the likes of' *26*: 5078, 425, 39, 4938.

Numeral. Cardinals are *uno 20*: 5078, 39 (it is not clear whether *una 46*: 4938, 235 is intended as the numeral 'one' or the indefinite article 'an'), *nweb(e) 20*: 5078, 39, 4938, *kwaranta 7*: 5078, 4938 [17] beside *kwarenta 7*: 39, *sinsyentoš 38*: 5078, 4938 [18] and *šey(š)syentoš 28*: 425, 39 (note the deletion of the alveolar *s* before the following dental). Ordinals are *primer-o, -a 6*: 5078, 39, 4938 (the *-o* is not apocopated in proclitic position: *el primero tokido 6*: 4938), and *šegunda 7*: 5078, 39, 25, 4938 [19].

Adjective. Present and past participles are frequently pressed into service as adjectives: *voz rretiemblante 8*: 235, *mano rrelunbrante 20*: 25; *tornada mintroša perdida 12*: 4938, *vistas humilladas 9*: 235. Two adjectives are joined without an intervening conjunction —probably imitating Arabic usage— in *bištaš temerošaš enklinadaš 9*: 39 and *tornada mintroša perdida 12*: 4938 [*Alj. T.*, 114-117]. A noun is used adjectivally in *pyedra kreštal 20*: 4938. The only comparative adjective is *mayor 20, 34*: 5078, 425, 39; the comparative phrase *de maš fwerte ẖaleqamyento 27*: 5078, 25, 4938 seems to be an awkward rendering of the Arabic *ashaddu khalqan* (lit. 'stronger as to creation'). All adjectives are postposed, except *fwerte* in the phrase just quoted and again in *fwerte fortuna mayor 34*: 4938 where a second adjective follows the noun. Note the separation of an adjective from its noun by an intervening prepositional phrase in *el šoflo de la tronpa sagero 34*: 4938.

Verb. All forms which occur for each verb in the text are listed in the Glossary under their respective infinitives. Here we will point out those forms and usages of special interest.

(D)ešmentir is the only 3rd conjugation verb which raises the stem vowel *e* to *i* before yod: *dešmintyo 21*: 25, *ešmintyo 21*: 5078, 39, 4938 (and *ešmintyendo 12*: 4938).

No strong past participles appear in the text; weak past participles end in *-ado* or *-ido*. Note *ḫaleqado 10*: 5078, 425 formed on *ḫaleqar* 'to create' < Ar. *khalaqa*.

Ser shows the 3rd singular preterite forms *fušte 45*: 4938[20] and *fwešte 45*: 425, 39 [*Batallas*, 59].

In the future tense, *detendra 40*: 235 exhibits loss of the stem vowel *e* with epenthesis of a dental; in *berna 34*: 25 (*venir*) loss of the vowel has been followed by metathesis, in contrast to *benrra 34*: 425 [*Batallas*, 30-31]. (For *trayran* see p. 32 above.) The personal pronoun is inserted between the elements of the periphrastic future in *demandarte an 42*: 25, 235, *(d)eškubriršе a 36*: 5078, 39, 25, 235, *gyarte a 19*: 5078, 425, 39, and *pareçerseles a 46*: 235; most of these examples have counterparts in which the pronoun is not intercalated.

The two instances of inchoative verbs are *akaeska 26*: 5078, 425, 39 (flanked by *akaesyó 26*: 5078, 425, 39), and *eškareskó 29*: 4938, in which the *-sk-* infix has apparently spread by analogy to the preterite (but cf. in the same passage *eškuresyó 29*: 5078, 39).

The Ĕ of *debeda 40:* 25 fails to diphthongize, probably under pressure of unstressed forms such as *debedará 40*: 5078, 39; that diphthongization did once occur in this verb is confirmed by *debyeda* (in a passage of BN 4938 not included in this study: fol. 58r 7). Note also the analogical spread of the diphthong to an unstressed syllable in *rretiemblante 7*: 235 [*P. Yúçuf*, 80; *Batallas*, 54].

The 1st plural present indicative of *aber* occurs both as *(h)abemoš 10*: 4938, 235) and as reduced *emoš* (*10*: 5078, 39, 25).

The 2nd plural present indicative of *ser* shows a range of developments: simple loss of *-d-* in *šoeš 27*: 4938 (the texts never preserve *-d-* in this form of the verb), closing of the unstressed vowel in *šoyš 27*: 39, 25, and loss of the semivowel in *šos* [*sic*] *27*: 5078. In the latter form, note the development -TIS > *[ts] > [s]; cf. *lebantaç, ayaç* [*R. Ališ.*, 459].

The 3rd plural preterite in *-oron* so characteristic of both Leonese and Aragonese is found in *še adebantor*[*o*]*n 4*: 5078 and *demandoron 42*: 4938 [*P. Yúçuf*, 83; *R. Ališ.*, 460; *Batallas*, 55] (although *demandoron* may be a copyist's error; see below, p. 43).

Ešpandó 30: 4938 loses the yod of the preterite (beside *ešpandyó 30*: 5078, 39), perhaps by analogy to the *-ar* class.

Strong -SI perfects are *konprišo 25*: 5078 and *mišo 32*: 5078. The perfect stem has spread to the gerund in *kišyendo 12*: 39, beside *keryendo 12*: 5078 (cf. *ubiʸendo, Batallas* 56). In a contrary development, the present stem contaminates the perfect in *abyešen* (imperf. subj.) *45*: 425 [*P. Yúçuf*, 80-81; *R. Ališ.*, 460-461; *Batallas*, 56]. Such confusion of present and perfect stem is a common Aragonese characteristic[21].

Imperitaves include *aw 19*: 5078 from *aber* (for the final consonant see above, p. 33), beside *abe 19*: 425, and *beš 17*: 5078, 39, 25, 4938 from *ir*; *ves* for *ve* is common in substandard Peninsular Spanish today.

Verbs are used reflexively with no apparent difference in meaning from the non-reflexive form in *še leš pareserá 46*: 4938, *pareçerseles a 46*: 235, in contrast to *leš paresera(n) 46*: 25, 39; in *še parten 1*: 5078, vs. *parten 1*: 25, 4938, 235; and in *še šegirá 7*: 25 vs. *seguirá 7*: 235. *Š-era 20*: 4938, *še rrekordará 35*: 5078, 39, 25, 4938, and *še rretornará 7*: 4938 would not be reflexive in modern usage. A reflexive occasionally has passive meaning: *(d)eškubrirše a ğahannam 36*: 5078, 39, 25, *še tokará 6*: 5078, 425, 39, *še klama 16*: 4938. (For questionable *šalboše,* see the Glossary.)

A past participle has active meaning in *deškonosido 37*: 25, 39 'unbelieving' [*R. Ališ.,* 464].

El šaber 44: 39, 425, 235 and *el plegar 44*: 25 are the only infinitives employed as nouns [*R. Ališ.,* 464].

In sentences containing a subordinate relative or temporal clause, the preferred tense is the future indicative in both main and subordinate clauses. Some examples from J 25: *el día ke še tokará la bozina ... abra korasoneš akel dia tinblanteš 6, 8; kwando berna la fortuna mayor ... el dia ke še rrekordará la peršona de lo ke abra obrado y-eškubrirše a ğahannam ... a kwanto kyen šera deškonosido y abantallará la bida de akešte mundo, pweš el fwego šerá šu šošyego 34-39; el dia ke lo beran no leš paresera ke fweron en el mundo ... 46* [*Alj. T.,* 61-65]. In two instances the result is expressed in the present indicative (*pweš el fwego eš [šu] šošyego 39*: 39, *pweš el alğanna[h] eš [šu] šošyego 41*: 39, 25), but all these constructions show an avoidance of the subjunctive as a means of expressing a hypothetical future. While in modern Spanish one would expect a present subjunctive ("cuando se toque la bocina", "el día que lo vean", etc.), the sixteenth-century language would probably have favored the future subjuntive ("tocare", "vieren"). Substitution of the future indicative in subordinate clauses of hypothetical futurity, in deliberate avoidance of the subjunctive, may be an Aragonese dialectal trait [22].

Another example of a relative clause shows a variation in use of mood: *pedrikador a kyen teme ada Allah 45*: 25 vs. *monestador a quien tema al dia del judiçio 45*: 235.

In a temporal clause, *depweš de šeyer 11*: 4938 contrasts with *depweš ke še(y)amoš 11*: 5078, 39, 25.

The verb *tener* does not occur in these texts. *Aber* is used in the modern sense of *tener* 'to have, possess' in the phrase *aber myedo 19*: 5078, 4938 *et passim* [*R. Ališ.,* 464]. *Aber de* plus infinitive may imply obligation or necessity (*¿aun emoš de šer rebibkadoš ...? 10*: 39), but elsewhere seems to have the sense of a simple future, as in *kwando a de šer šu rrefirmamyento 42*: 25 (cf. *kwando šera šu rrefirmamyento 42*: 39) [23].

Ser is used impersonally, with the meaning 'to occur', in *i apreš d-ella šera la šegund[a] [tokada] 7*: 5078 [*R. Ališ.,* 464]. (The apparently parallel construction *no šera šino un tokamyento en la bozina 13*: 4938, 5078 probably is not impersonal but rather means 'it will be', in view of the original Arabic *hiya zajratun wāhida.*) *Ser* has the meaning of modern *estar* in *šeran šobre la kara de la tyerra 14*: 5078 and *fweron en el mundo 46*: 4938, 39, 25 (cf. *estubieron en el mundo 46*: 235) [24].

An irregular subject-verb agreement occurs in *una pyedra kreštal ke rrapan la bišta de loš oğoš 20*: 4938, and in *no leš pareseran ke ... 46*: 425 where the plural pronoun apparently provoked a mistaken plural verb.

The verb *llegar* seems intended as transitive in *y llegó su gente 23*: 235 (cf. *i hizo llegar la ğente 23*: 39).

Adverb. The Aragonese form of the ending *-ment(e)* < -MENTĒ occurs in *berdaderament(e) 13*: 5078, 425, 4938, and *nwebament(e) 10*: 5078, 425, 4938; there is no trace in these passages of the common Old Castilian variants *-miente* and *-mientre*.

Preposition. Note especially *ada 19*: 5078, 39, 25, 235 *et passim; apreš de 7*: 5078, 425, 23, *30*: 5078, 425, 4938; *dakía 33*: 5078, 425; and *šinše 27*: 5078, 425, 25, *šineš (de) 27*: 4938 beside *šin 27*: 39 [*P. Yúçuf*, 85-86; *R. Ališ.*, 461; *Batallas*, 61-65]. Preposition usage is inconsistent in the texts, and one reason is surely the problem presented by translation: the Arabic of the Qur'ān can be highly compressed or elliptical, and a translator may choose from a variety of phrases with which to expand and clarify the meaning of the original. Note, for example, *(el mandamyento) ke kreyaš 18*: 5078, 425, vs. *en ke kreaš 18*: 39 or *a ke te alinpyeš 18*: 25; for other cases see below, p. 41. *A* appears before a non-personal direct object in *21*: 5078 and *40*: 425 [*R. Ališ.*, 463].

Conjunction. *I* or *y* is the form of the coordinating conjunction 'and' in the overwhelming majority of cases; *e* appears only eight times, half of them in BN 5078 [*Batallas*, 33]. Note *kar 26*: 4938 (cf. Fr. *car*, OSp. *ca*). As with the prepositions, usage is strongly influenced by the attempt to render the sense of the Arabic original; see below, pp. 41-42.

Word Formation.

Prefixes. The usage of the texts vacillates as to presence or absence of certain prefixes: *de-bedar 40*: 5078, 425, vs. *bedar 40*: 4938; *por-paramyento 40*: 5078, 39, 25 as against *paramyento 40*: 4938. The presence of such pairs as *a-debantarše 4*: 5078 / *debantarše 4*: 425 may have contributed to the apheresis in *bantallar 38*: 5078 (cf. *abantallar 38*: 425, 39, *abantağar 38*: 4938 < Fr. *avantage*). Characteristic of Aragonese is the alternation between *des-* (< DIS-, DE ĘX-) and *es-* (< ĘX-) without change of meaning[25], and these texts are no exception: *deš-, eš-kubrirše 36, deš-, eš-mentir 12, 21, deš-, eš-pleyte 33*; in the set *deššenplo/ exemplo/inš(y)emplo 26* a third prefix, IN-, even enters the equation, probably attracted by the existing nasal. The variants *pre-, per-šona 35, 40,* the former also frequent in Aragonese[26], owe their coexistence as much to the competing Latin prefixes PRAE- and PER- as to simple metathesis[27].

Suffixes. As has frequently been noted in studies of translations from both Arabic and Hebrew into Spanish[28], the resulting Romance texts show a high proportion of neologisms, particularly deverbal abstract nouns, coined in the effort to render precise shades of meaning of the Semitic original. In our texts as elsewhere, the suffix overwhelmingly favored for such cases is *-myento* (52 occurrences). Deverbals are also formed with *-ado* or *-ada* (*parada 40*: 235) and *-ura* (*andadura 28*).

Sound-suffixes exist in an unusually high concentration here: beside *tok-ada 6*: 5078 and *tok-amyento 7*: 5078 we find *rretronido 6*: 235, *soflido 13*: 235 and *tokido 6, 7*: 4938, all with the meaning 'note, blast' (on a trumpet). None of the last three is recorded in a published inventory of sound-formations in *-ido*[29].

-Ada is used denominally to form *begada 34*: 5078, 425, and *mannanada 46*: 4938. Nouns are formed from adjectives by *-ansa* (*umildansa 9*: 25) and *-eza*

(*alteza 28*: 425). *-Illo, -yello* is the only form of diminutive suffix. *-Aryo* (*altaryo 28*: 4938) is a learned replacement for *-ero* < -ARIU [30].

In a few cases, Romance verbal or nominal endings are attached directly to Arabic bases: Ar. *khalaqa* 'to create' becomes *ḫaleqar 10*: 4938 'id.', and is flanked by *ḫaleqado* and *ḫaleqamyento*; the plurals *almalakeš 2, 4*: 5078, 425 'angels' and *arruḥeš 2*: 5078, 425, 'souls' are formed on the Arabic nouns *malak* and *rūḥ*, respectively [*Alj. T.*, 69-81].

Special Syntactic Features.

Any text translated from a foreign language will inevitably exhibit, to a greater or lesser degree depending on the translator's skill, influence of the source language in wording or syntax. Studies of the translations from Arabic into Spanish made under the aegis of Alfonso X in the thirteenth century have demonstrated how the texts were gradually "purified" of their Semitic elements: while early versions of a text may show a heavily Arabized syntax, successive recensions are gradually freed from dependence on their model, until the resulting prose bears only minimal signs of its origin [31]. In Aljamiado translations of the Qur'ān, however, not only is no attempt made to de-Semiticize the syntax, but the contrary is actually true: reverence for the language of the original makes the translators depart as little as possible from Arabic modes of expression. In this section we shall identify, classify, and analyze the syntactic features in our six Qur'ān MSS which seem to owe some debt to Arabic. This is not to say that they may not exist independently of Arabic, for some are found in other Romance languages and in Latin; nonetheless their heavy concentration in these texts betrays an especially direct reliance on the language of the Qur'ān.

Parataxis. The repeated linking of main clauses by a simple conjunction such as "and" is one of the most notable features of early (Alfonsine) Castilian prose and has long been recognized as a trait imitated from Arabic. The latter language, having no punctuation or capitalization, puts the conjunctions *wa* and *fa* to use virtually as Western languages do the period, to mark the end of a complete idea and the beginning of a new one. The paratactic style is the norm in the Aljamiado versions of *Sūrat an-Nāziᶜāt,* so much so that the conjunctions *i* or *e* outnumber their Arabic counterparts. Of the forty-six verses in the chapter, nineteen begin with a coordinating *wa* or *fa* in Arabic; but in BN 4938 twenty-six start with *i* or *e,* in J 25 twenty-five, in T 235 twenty-three. Clearly, for the translators, the conjunction has become a convenient crutch to lean on. Undoubtedly Qur'ānic language relies less on parataxis than does standard Classical Arabic prose, because the end-rhyme of each verse serves to mark the completion of a thought, thus making a conjunction redundant. The translations, lacking the signal of rhyme, naturally would need to make the linkage more explicit. See, for example, a sequence like verses 6-9, in which the Arabic does without conjunctions entirely: *yawma tarjufu r-rājifa / tatbaᶜuhā r-rādifa / qulūbun yawma'idhin wājifa / abṣāruhā khāshiᶜa.* In every case an Aljamiado translation links the clauses with *i*: (J 25) *el dia ke še tokará la bozina, i apreš d-ella še šegira la šegunda tokada* (P 425) *i abrá korasoneš en akel dia tenblanteš,* (J 25) *i šuš bištaš temerošaš kon umildansa* [*P. Yúçuf*, 88].

Paranomasia. In this construction, also known as "cognate accusative", the verb and its direct object share the same root; Arabic morphology particularly favors the usage (e. g., *ḍarabahu ḍarban* 'he hit him (hard)', lit. 'he hit him a hitting'). Though paranomasia does occur independently in Romance, it increases greatly in frequency in texts translated from Arabic; in our Aljamiado MSS it appears, like parataxis, even where it is not present in the Arabic original. We may distinguish, in the Aljamiado, between "true" and "false" paranomasia: in the former, as required by the original Arabic, the verbal noun is always the direct object of its verb; in the latter it may be some other element of the sentence (usually the subject), but the two types share a strong superficial resemblance. Verses 2-4 of Sūra 79 contain a series of cognate accusatives (of which the first element is not actually a verb, but an active participle used with verbal force) that T 235 renders literally: *por los arrancantes arrancamiento, por los andantes andamiento, por los adelantantes adelantamiento.* These are, in fact, the only true paranomastic constructions in the Arabic text, yet the Morisco translators, apparently captivated by the Spanish equivalent, employ it elsewhere: *i alsó ... su altura 28*: 25. "False" paranomasia, especially, abounds: *še tokará ... la primera tokada 6*: 5078, 425 (the Arabic original suggests that the noun is the subject here), *un tokamiento ... šera tokado 13*: 25, *rretronarán los rretronidos 6*: 235; perhaps also *ke-l tomarán konto de šuš obraš de lo ke abrá obrado 35*: 5078. The density of such constructions in such a relatively brief text suggests considerable familiarity with Arabic models [*Alj. T.*, 105-107; *Batallas*, 89-92].

Anacoluthon. More informally known as the "topic-comment" construction, this usage consists in placing the direct-object noun before the verb, then repeating it after the verb in pronominal form. Both examples from Sūra 79 occur in verses in which the Arabic employs the same construction. At verse 30 (*wa-l-arḍa baᶜda dhālika daḥāhā*), three MSS translate literally, while the other three change the word order to avoid anacoluthon: compare J 25's *i la tyerra depweš de akello eštendyola* with BN 5078's *y-ešpandyo apreš de akello la tyerra.* At verse 32, all six MSS agree with the Arabic: *wa-l-jibāla arsāhā* becomes *i lòš monteš pušološ rrefirmamyento* (P 425). *El syelo ke lo frag(w)ó 27*: 5078, 425, 39 may be called "false" anacoluthon, since in the Arabic the noun is the subject (nominative case), not the direct object (accusative) as the "true" construction requires. Compare this phenomenon with the "false" paranomasia described above [*R. Ališ.*, 463-464; *Alj. T.*, 120-123; *Batallas*, 93-94].

Relative clauses. For the several categories of relativization in Arabic, the Aljamiado translations find a variety of solutions:

Mā 'what': *lo ke 35*: all.

Man 'who, whom': *kyen* after a preposition *26, 36*: all, *45*: 25, 4938, 235; *kyen* as subject *40*: 5078, 425, *45*: 425, 39?, and as subject after *a kwanto* 'as for' *37*: all, *40*: 425, 39, 25, 4938. These results differ from Galmés' observation that the commonest translation of *man* is *el/la/lo que*; he finds two examples in his Alfonsine text of *quien* after prepositions, but none of this relative alone [32].

Asyndetic relative: Arabic, as a highly synthetic language, abounds in relative constructions which do not employ any pronoun; thus the Aljamiado translations must supply one in order to form a coherent sentence. One of the commonest Arabic usages involves use of the *ᶜā'id* or "returning" pronoun which restates the antecedent, e. g. *huwa ar-rajulu ra'aituhu amsi*, lit. 'he is the man I saw him yesterday' ('he is the man whom I saw yesterday'). Sūra 79 contains one such construction at verse *27*, *as-samā'u banāhā* 'the heaven which He built' (lit. 'the heaven He built it'): the Aljamiado versions add the relative pronoun, *el syelo ke lo frag*[*w*]*ó*. This *ᶜā'id* construction may even be used in Aljamiado where the

Arabic omits it, as in verse 5: *por loš almalakeš ke ... rriǧe Allah kon elloš lo ke kyere,* lit. 'by the angels who ... God rules with them what he wills', as opposed to the normal Spanish construction **loš almalakeš kon kyen[eš] rriǧe Allah ...* [*R. Ališ.*, 463; *Alj. T.*, 137-142; *Batallas*, 67-69].

The series of Arabic active participles in verses 1-5 (*an-nāziᶜāti, an-nāshiṭāti, as-sābiḥāti,* etc.) is particularly difficult to translate literally. Each participle, though itself a noun, has enough verbal force to take a direct object; the resulting two-word clause is so compressed, both syntactically and semantically, that any translation must involve considerable expansion or paraphrase. All the Aljamiado versions render these participal constructions with relative clauses introduced by *ke*. *Wa-n-nāziᶜāti gharqan*, lit. 'by the pluckers with a (single) pull', thus becomes *por laš estrellaš ke še parten; wa-n-nāshiṭāti nashṭan,* lit. 'by the pullers pulling', becomes *por loš almalakes ke arrankan,* and so forth. Galmés[33] considers such Arabic constructions as examples of relativization by means of the definite article (rather than by a relative pronoun). However, as the Aljamiado translations here show, the relative clause is not at all implicit in the original Arabic, but rather arises in Spanish out of the attempt to render the sense of an active participle which happens to be definite[34].

The *mā ... min* partitive construction forms another category of Arabic relative clauses, of the type *hādhā mā-shtaraituhu min aṭ-ṭaᶜāmi,* lit. 'this is what I bought it of food', i. e. 'this is the food that I bought'. One example occurs in the Arabic of Sūra 79, but the sense is rather interrogative than relative (verse 43, *fīmā anta min dhikrāhā,* lit. 'what are you concerned with of its mention?'), and no relative clause appears in the translation. At verse 36, however, the Aljamiado has created a partitive construction where the Arabic had none, rendering a simple *man ra'ā* 'whoever sees' as *kyen bera de loš maloš* [*R. Ališ.*, 465; *Batallas,* 102-103].

Remaining instances of relative clauses in the Aljamiado texts have no exact counterpart in the Arabic Qur'ān; in general, they arise from attempts to expand a highly synthetic Arabic construction by means of a paraphrase. Such are, for example, phrases that translate the adverb of time *yawma* 'on the day' as *el día ke* (*še tokará*) *6*: 5078, 425, 39, *el día ke* (*še rrekordará*) *35*: 5078, 39, 25.

Omission of verbal copula. Aljamiado occasionally imitates this trait of Arabic, a language which does not express the verb 'to be' in the present tense. Verse 7: 4938 has *i entre ell un tokido i ell otro kwaranta annoš* (other MSS supply *abrá* before *kwaranta,* but comparison with the Arabic commentaries proves that 4938's is not an accidental omission). In verse 9, *i šuš bištaš temerošaš* 39, 25, *i loš oǧoš de akelloš amedresidoš* 4938, match the Arabic *abṣāruhā khāshiᶜa* (no copula); 5078 and 425 supply *šeran.* Understandably, however, since omission of the copula runs counter to Romance practice, the translation may supply the verb where it is absent in Arabic. Therefore *ser* has been added in verses 39 and 41 [*R. Ališ.*, 465; *Alj. T.*, 123-127; *Batallas,* 94-95].

"To have" expressed by a preposition. Arabic expresses the action of possessing not by a verb but rather by a preposition (most often *ᶜinda* or *li* followed by the personal pronoun, e. g., *ᶜindī* 'I have' (lit. 'to me [is]'), *mā lī* 'I have not' (lit. '[there is] not to me'). Our Aljamiado texts translate such phrases literally, supplying the verb 'to be'. *Eš a tī 18*: 4938, *a tu es 18*: 235 both render Ar. *laka.* A possible third case occurs in verse 44, where the preposition *ilā* is taken by some of the MSS to imply possession: *ada Allah eš el saber* 425, 39 probably means "God [alone] possesses the knowledge". Yet, as *ilā*'s basic meaning is of motion rather than possession, the alternate translation *a tu šennor eš el plegar* (25)

suggests an interpretation such as, "it is to God that you shall arrive in the end" [*Alj. T.*, 117-118; *Batallas,* 96].

The SER ... -DOR *construction.* The Arabic active participle partakes of the dual nature of verb and noun; it may take an object either in the accusative or in the genitive. *Rajulun qātilu n-nāsi,* lit. 'a man a killer of people', would generally be translated by a verb in English, i. e., 'a man who kills people'. Aljamiado, however, often takes the Arabic usage at face value, and translates with an agentive noun in *-dor,* the closest equivalent to the Arabic participle [35]. One clear example of the phenomenon occurs in our texts in verse *45*: 425: *I tu no fweš[te] enbyado šino pedrikador ke abyešen myedo,* rendering Ar. *mundhiru man yakhshāhā;* the intended meaning is "fuiste enviado *para predicar* que tuviesen miedo". In the same passage in the other MSS, *pre(d)i-, pedrikador* also represents the verbal idea, "el que predica" [*Batallas,* 84-85]. (The *no* ... *sino* construction itself is probably suggested by Arabic usage: *Batallas,* 96-98).

Uses of the conjunction I. Arabic *fa* serves not only as the coordinating conjunction, 'and', but also as a disjunctive, adversative, or subordinating one, and to introduce the apodosis in a conditional sentence. Thus the Spanish *y,* in translations from Arabic, tends to expand its semantic range and to take over some of these additional functions of *fa.* In Sūra *79,* the Aljamiado translations employ *i* (*y*) in such expanded senses in several verses in place of Ar. *fa. I* has consecutive meaning ('and so, therefore') in verse 25: the sequence *fa-qāla anā rabbukum* ... *fa-akhadhahu-llah* 'and he said, "I am your Lord ...", so God seized him' becomes *i dišo, "Yo šo bweštro šennor ..." i konprišolo Allah* (5078) [*P. Yúçuf,* 88; *Alj. T.*, 157-159; *Batallas,* 88]. At verse 21, *i/y* is employed in place of an adversative *fa*: *fa-arāhu l-āyata* ... *fa-kadhdhaba* 'so He showed him the sign. ... but he denied [it]' is translated *i demoštrole* ... *y-esmintyo* (5078), treating both *fa*'s as if they were equivalent in meaning [*P. Yúçuf,* 88]. The considerable subtleties in the usage of this particular Arabic particle evidently were not always clear to the Morisco translator.

Preposition usage. The tendency to translate too literally from Arabic produces in Aljamiado combinations of verb plus preposition which are not characteristic of the standard language. *Kreer kon 18*: 39, *38*: 5078 'to believe in' recalls Ar. *āmana bi,* although the latter phrase does not actually appear in this Qur'ānic text. Similarly, *konprender kon* with the meaning 'to punish" (verse 25) harks back to *ākhadha bi* 'id.', even though the Arabic verse here omits the preposition, employing instead a noun of instrument. The fact that both these verb-preposition combinations appear in an Aljamiado text without any direct Arabic model shows that, although originating in literal translation, they had by this time become independent common usages in their own right.

The Arabic preposition *fī* may refer to location, and mean 'in' or 'on', but has an additional meaning of 'about', 'concerning' (the sense of English 'on' in "this is a book on gardening"). In Aljamiado, therefore, *en* may mean 'about' when it stands for Ar. *fī.* The phrase *en ella dixo 13*: 235, though not originating in the Qur'ān but probably in exegesis, appears to mean 'he said concerning (on the subject of) it'. In verse 43, Ar. *fīmā anta,* admittedly difficult to translate, becomes in Aljamiado *en ke-štaš tu*?, implying "what do you have to do with it?". *Fī* here is obviously within the semantic range of 'concerning' [*R. Ališ.*, 462-463; *Alj. T.*, 89-100, 118-120; *Batallas,* 99-102].

Usage of I, PWES, *and* KE. The Morisco translators of the Qur'ān faced a special challenge: to make a coherent, connected narrative out of an Arabic text that did not lend itself to such treatment. The language of the Qur'ān is a rhymed prose of extraordinary sonority and evocative power. Each verse, which may vary in length from two words to as many as fifty —in Sūra 79 the average is only 3.8— expresses a thought that is syntactically and semantically complete, and that ends in the anticipated, recurrent beat of the rhyme sound. Since this rhythm and rhyme give the prose such a strong feeling of continuity, connective words like coordinating and subordinating conjunctions lose importance and are not extensively employed.

The Aljamiado translations, however, do need to replace the lost rhyme with devices which will make clear the logical relationships between individual verses; hence their reliance on conjunctions. We have already spoken of the paratactic use of *i*. More subtle are the subordinating conjunctions *pweš* and *ke*. The former most often translates Ar. *fa*: it is semantically almost empty (roughly 'well, now') in *13*: 5078, 39, 25, *27*: 25, 4938, *34*: 39, 25; has consecutive meaning ('then, therefore') in *19*: 5078, 425 (as demonstrated by the parallel translation of *para ke* plus subjunctive in *19*: 4938, 235); and introduces the result after *a kwanto* (Ar. *ammā ... fa*) in *39, 41*: all. Arabic has no conjunction in verse 43, which P 425 and J 39 link to the previous one with *pweš* [*Alj. T.*, 151-156].

It is even clearer that the translators employ the conjunction *ke* as a useful connector where their Arabic original provides no syntactic link between verses. This *ke*, chiefly asseverative or emphatic, is virtually untranslatable. In the handful of cases where it stands for the Arabic intensifying particle *inna* (*17*: 5078, 39, 25; *26*: 235) it might be rendered 'indeed'. But generally it has been supplied, in the absence of any Arabic equivalent, to create a transition between two ideas, and to mean approximately 'for': "*... el bal šanto de Ṭuwā*", *ke ašī še kl*[*am*]*a akel monte 16*: 4938; *i konprendyolo Allah kon la pena del otro mundo i de akešte, ke lo afogó en la mar 25*: 25; *que alçó su sostenimiento 28*: 235. Thus the conjunction allows to the text some degree of logical continuity, where the Arabic original, able to rely on the unifying effect of rhyme, does not always supply strong semantic links between verses.

Relative chronology of the MSS. We have described the most significant features of our six MSS taken as a whole, so as to paint a comprehensive picture of the language of the Aljamiado translations of the Qur'ān. Such treatment *en masse* is justified in the case of a group of texts so closely allied both in spirit and in execution. Yet each MS was composed or copied at its own time and place, and the language of each may be the only clue to its date and area of origin. Therefore we will attempt to establish a relative chronology of the six MSS —an absolute chronology would be very difficult— on the basis of their phonological and morphological features.

The conclusions of this attempt must necessarily be tentative ones. Within each MS, Sūra 79 occupies only a handful of folios, and the remaining ones do not enter into our calculations: they might conceivably contain bits of evidence more conclusive than those we are examining. This disadvantage constitutes, of course, the corollary to the advantage of limiting the material under study to a reasonable amount. Further studies will, in all likelihood, uncover limitations and call for shifts of emphasis. Here we hope merely to make our conclusions valid for the evidence that we do present.

A second caveat, more significant than the first, arises from our ignorance of *both* the spatial and the temporal origin of these MSS. The Moriscos dwelt in significant numbers in nearly every part of the Iberian Peninsula except the extreme northwest. Wherever they lived they spoke and wrote the local dialect, unless they had been forcibly resettled outside their native territory, as happened to the Moriscos of Granada after the rebellion of 1570-71. Yet it has been surmised that, living in relative isolation as they often did, their speech may have retained certain archaic traits already abandoned by their Christian neighbors [36]. And some of these traits cross dialect boundaries: that is to say that what in Castilian was an archaism, like preservation of the -D- in *piedes,* represented normal contemporary usage in Aragonese. On discovering that MS A consistently shows *piedes* and MS B *pies,* we might reasonably conclude either 1) that A antedates B, and that both originated in Castile, or 2) that the two are contemporary, but A is of Aragonese, and B of Castilian, provenance. The problem of this interplay of "age and area" has no absolute solution. Therefore we may at times have to content ourselves with the tentative conclusion that a given feature is either more archaic or more dialectal than another, without being able to decide between the two. Only a handful of traits belong incontestably only to Aragonese, and these will be especially useful indicators.

On the basis of all the phonological and morphological evidence, the two BN MSS, 5078 and 4938, are unquestionably the earliest of the six texts. Both exhibit the following features found both in Aragonese and in Old Castilian: loss of *-e* after *nt*; preservation of F- (except for a single *h-* in BN 4938); preservation of -D-; *-d* devoiced to *-t*. BN 4938 contains in addition: *we* unreduced to *e* (*kulwebra*) and unmetathesized *miraglo*. Of traits that may be assigned definitely to Aragonese, the two texts share: *ye* unreduced before a palatal; failure to diphthongize stressed Ŏ (*konto*); *kwaranta* < *QUARÁENTA; initial *pl-, kl-*. Only BN 4938 preserves a -T-, in *gayata*; but only BN 5078 shows CT > [*i̯t*], and consistently diphthongizes before *yod*. (BN 5078's one instance of Ŏ > *wa,* sharply isolated, could easily result from a scribal error.) On the basis of phonology, then, we conclude that both MSS convey a noticeable Aragonese flavor, BN 5078 slightly more so in the light of the forms *nwey* and *wellos̆*; BN 4938's single *h-* points to a more recent date.

The morphological evidence is more conclusive. BN 5078's locution *la otro* finds a parallel elsewhere in Aragonese. In the verb, both MSS consistently employ the anti-hiatic *y* in *šeyer,* and use *šo* as the first singular of the present indicative; both permit separation of the two elements of the periphrastic future. But only BN 5078 exhibits the more archaic conjunction *e,* and the Aragonese traits of the present subjunctive *šia* and the imperative *aw*. The fact that both texts contain a preterite in *-oron* is probably illusory: the form from BN 4938, *demandoron,* occurs in a verse in which all the other MSS have a future tense, and is thus likely to be an error for *demandarán*. *Še adebantor[o]n* in BN 5078, on the other hand, is a genuine preterite, and as such provides strong evidence for the more Aragonese character, and hence the earlier date, of this MS.

Our chronological order, then, can begin with BN 5078 and BN 4938 as the two oldest texts; the former takes precedence on the basis of the greater number and purity of its Aragonese forms. The MS which we have previously identified as the "sister" of BN 5078 is P 425 (both are copies of a common original), but the genetic relationship of the two texts does not in this case imply a contemporary date. P 425 must have been copied in Aragon as well, but considerably later than BN 5078. Assuming that the latter reflects faithfully the language of its model, then the scribe of P 425 must have deliberately modernized the text. P 425 reduces *ye* to *i* before a palatal; accentuates *QUARAÉNTA > *kwarenta*; preserves *-e* after *nt*; loses -D- (*ǧwisyo*); and suppresses anti-hiatic -*y*-. At the same time, other features establish its Aragonese origin: diphthongization before *yod* and CT > [*i̯t*] in *nweyte* (note the -*e*, as against *nwey* in BN 5078)[37]; preservation of PL-, CL-, and F-; metathesized *pedrikador*. In the verb, P 425 modernizes in employing *šoyš* beside BN 5078's *šos, pušo* beside *mišo, šea* beside *šia, abe* beside *aw*. Yet it betrays its Aragonese filiation in the future *benrra*; in the imperfect subjunctive *abyešen*, which shows contamination by the present stem; and in the gerund *kišyendo*, in which the perfect stem replaces the present. Obviously, therefore, P 425 belongs to a different chronological layer from its sister MS BN 5078. It was copied in Aragon, but at a period in which the Castilianization of the Aragonese dialect was much advanced. Before assigning it a definite place in the chronology, we shall proceed to the evaluation of the two Almonacid MSS, J 39 and J 25.

These two texts differ most sharply from each other in their treatment of F- and of the PL- and CL- clusters. J 25 preserves all three consistently, while J 39 changes F- to *h*- and the clusters to *ll*- throughout. On this evidence alone, J 39 is clearly the more recent of the two. This MS also avoids antihiatic *y*. All of these features could point to Castilian provenance, but there are reasons to believe that J 39 is actually of Aragonese origin, though of a late date. Like P 425, which we have shown to be Aragonese, it forms the gerund *kišyendo* with a perfect stem. Further, J 39 is the only one of the six MSS to lose a final -*o*, in *mintroš*; however, such an isolated form must be viewed with suspicion, as it could very easily represent a scribal error. A final argument for suspecting that J 39 is Aragonese is merely circumstantial, the fact of its having been discovered at Almonacid de la Sierra in the province of Zaragoza. Although the MSS of that cache numbered in the hundreds, and could therefore have been collected from different places over a long period of time, nonetheless the great bulk were probably of local origin.

J 25, in contrast, belongs to an older layer by virtue of its retention of F-, PL-, and CL-. Its Aragonese origin shows in such forms as the preposition *parad*, which retains the etymological final consonant before a following vowel, and in the metathesized future verb *berná*.

As best can be determined, then, the chronology of the five MSS discussed so far runs as follows: BN 5078, BN 4938, P 425, J 25, J 39. The third and fourth in this series are particularly difficult to date relative to each other, but since P 425 has a slight edge in features recognizably Aragonese (CT > *i̯t*, -*d* > -*t*, gerund *kišyendo*), we consider it earlier than J 25.

By almost any linguistic criterion, T 235, the only text written in Latin script, is the latest of all the MSS. The date of 1606 that the MS bears is suggestive, yet a close reading of the marginal notes reveals that this MS was copied from an earlier one which was probably in Arabic letters[38]. The scribe, unfortunately, does not reveal his place of origin, but his language, if not one hundred percent Castilian, is highly Castilianized. He asserts repeatedly that he has copied his model exactly, word for word (*esta rrectamente kopyado como lo halló*), changing only the alphabet in which it was written; and if these statements are true, then the original MS must have belonged to the latter years of the sixteenth century, for its language is more recent than that of any of the other five texts. T 235 reduces *ie* to *i* before a palatal; converts PL-, CL- to *ll*- and F- to *h*-; avoids velarization in *huesos*, as against *gwešoš* in the other five MSS; shows *ch* for original -CT-. In the verb it displays such standard forms as *soy, sois, vendrá*. Of course it is partly the Latin script of this one text that contributes to its air of "modernity"; it is, for example, the only MS capable of displaying orthographic confusions such as *b* for *v* (*estubieron 46*) and substitution of one sibilant for another (*deçian 10, alteça 28*). The latter are particularly useful in dating the text after the devoicing of Old Spanish *-z-*, and probably at a time when the sibilant shift was fully accomplished.

Late though T 235 may be, however, and much as its language shows influence of the dominant Castilian, it still reveals in a handful of forms the residual Aragonese speech habits of its author or scribe. Among these are the form of the preposition *ad* before a vowel (*ada Allah 19*; *tu* as object of a preposition (*a tu es 18*); and the noun *fuesas* (*10*) with characteristic diphthong. On the lexical side one may adduce the gerund *esbuludreando* (*8*), whose nearest relatives belong to the Provençal-Catalan group.

If, then, we evaluate once more the language of these six MSS in its entirety, we are left with an impression of an Aragonese speech in constant retreat vis-à-vis the increasingly dominant Castilian. Even the two texts which we deem the earliest chronologically, BN 5078 and BN 4938, show considerable Castilian admixture; the latter, in particular, reads *noče* and *oǧoš,* and changes F- to *h-* in a single instance. Through P 425 and J 25, the balance shifts increasingly away from Aragonese, until in the two latest MSS, J 39 and T 235, the Castilian takeover is virtually accomplished: initial *ll-* and *h-* throughout, no diphthongization before *yod,* and standard verb conjugations.

It may be useful, too, to recall how many linguistic features identified with Aragonese and found in earlier texts in that dialect do *not* appear in any of these Morisco Qur'ān translations. Some of these traits, occurring in the various *fueros* of the thirteenth and fourteenth centuries, are: diphthongized forms of verbs such as *yes, ye* from *ser, viengo* from *venir;* preservation of medial voiceless stops (except for the single form *gayata*); reduction of MB to *m;* preservation of Latin initial G-, J-; palatalization of L-; and hypercharacterization of gender in the *-e* adjectives (e. g., *tristo, granda*). Likewise the lexicon of the Aljamiado texts lacks such common Aragonese items as the adverbs *y* < IBI and *en* < INDE (found also in Old Castilian) the preposition *tro a,* possessives *lur, lures,* etc. If the Moriscos, living in relatively self-contained rural communities, felt the impact of the official national speech to this extent, then the language of Christian town-dwellers must have shed, by this period, even more of its dialectal flavor. Although any attempt at precise dating is fraught with hazards, it seems fairly safe to surmise that of these six Aljamiado texts the oldest probably does not precede 1520 [39], and the most recent, copied in 1606, may hark back to an original composed between 1580 and 1590.

NOTES.

1 See, e. g., the transliterations in J. Ribera and M. Asín, *Catálogo de los manuscritos árabes y aljamiados de la Biblioteca de la Junta* (Madrid, 1912).

2 "Aljamiado Literature: *El Rrekontamiʸento del Rrey Ališandᵉre*", *RH,* LXXVII (1929), 409-611.

3 J. R. Craddock, review of R. Kontzi, *Aljamiadotexte. Ausgabe mit einer Einleitung zur Sprache und Glossar,* 2 vols. (Wiesbaden, 1974); in *JAOS,* XCVIII: 4 (1978), 493-498.

4 Editorial Gredos, Madrid; three titles published to date: A. Galmés de Fuentes (ed.), *Historia de los amores de París y Viana* (1970) and *El libro de las batallas: Narraciones épico-caballerescas,* 2 vols. (1975); *Actas del Coloquio Internacional Sobre Literatura Aljamiada y Morisca* (1978).

[5] In the system established by A. Galmés for the Colección de Literatura Española Aljamiado-Morisca, *sīn* = *ç*, *shīn* = *s*, *shīn* with *tashdīd* = *x*. This representation of the sibilants is unsatisfactory on several grounds. First, two of the symbols used obey traditional Old Spanish orthography too closely: *ç* and *x*, phonetically [ts] and [š], respectively. Second, *ç* [ts] suggests an affricate pronunciation, yet there is no clear evidence that the occlusive element persisted as late as the sixteenth century. (Galmés himself cites, in *Batallas* II, 17, numerous instances of *s* for *ç*, e. g., *aderesaron, parese.*) Finally, *shīn* should be transcribed as a true palatal, [š], in the light of contemporary evidence that the Moriscos did in fact palatalize Spanish (apico-alveolar) *s* in their daily speech: as Nebrija claimed, "por lo que nosotros dezimos *señor san Simon* por *s*, [los moros] dizen *xeñor xan Ximon*, por *x*" (quoted in A. E. Sloman, "The Phonology of Moorish Jargon in the Works of Early Spanish Dramatists and Lope de Vega", *MLR*, XLIV [1949], 207-217).

[6] R. Menéndez Pidal, *Orígenes*; Alvar, *Dial.*, 151-152.

[7] For Ŏ > *ua* in Aragonese see Alvar, *ibid.*, 147-148.

[8] J. Fernández de Heredia, *La Grant Cronica de Espanya Libros I-II*, ed. R. af Geijerstam (Uppsala, 1964).

[9] *Vidal*, 26.

[10] The antihiatic -*y*- is an Aragonese characteristic: see B. Pottier, *AFA*, II (1947), 124-144.

[11] Cf. *trayer* in the *F. Teruel*, 39.

[12] *La fin* in Aragonese: Alvar, *Dial.*, 208.

[13] In a document of 1471: D. J. Gifford and F. W. Hodcroft, *Textos lingüísticos del medioevo español*, 2nd ed. (Oxford, 1966), 206.

[14] Menéndez Pidal, *Orígenes*, 401; Keniston, *Syntax*, 89 ff.

[15] Galmés, *Influencias*, 110; Keniston, *ibid.*, 90.

[16] *Vidal*, 35.

[17] From *QUARÁENTA, cf. Arag., It. *quaranta* (Alvar, *Dial.*, 211).

[18] *Cincientos* in Aragonese (*loc. cit.*).

[19] On the Aragonese numerals in general see B. Pottier, *AFA*, II (1947), 145-149.

[20] *Fušte*, if not an error, may go back to a *FUSTE < FUISTI: cf. *fot* reflecting the same change from FUIT, Huesca, 1095 (R. Menéndez Pidal, *Orígenes*, 365). The reading *fošte* is also possible.

[21] Alvar, *Dial.*, 246-247.

[22] Keniston, *op. cit.*, 438.

[23] *Haber* meaning possession or obligation survived longer in Aragon than in other regions of Spain: see E. Seifert, *RFE*, XVII (1930), 233-276, 342-389, esp. 384.

[24] Alternation of *ser* and *estar* is frequent in Aragonese: Alvar, *Dial.*, 293.

[25] *Vidal*, 26; *F. Teruel*, 39.

[26] G. W. Umphrey, *RH*, XXIV (1911), 29; *presonas* is cited only as evidence that "metathesis is very common in illiterate speech in Aragon".

[27] See Y. Malkiel, *RPh*, III (1949-40), 27-72.

[28] Kontzi, *Aljamiadotexte*, I, 79-80; J. Millás Vallicrosa, *And*, I (1933), 155-187, esp. 160-161.

[29] J. R. Craddock and E. Georges, *RPh*, XVII (1963-64), 87-107.

[30] A thorough recent treatment of this subject is D. G. Pattison's *Early Spanish Suffixes: A Functional Study of the Principal Nominal Suffixes of Spanish up to 1300*, Publications of the Philological Society, XXVII (Oxford, 1975).

[31] A. Galmés, *Influencias*, 10.

[32] *Ibid.*, 69.

[33] *Ibid.*, 77.

[34] Galmés acknowledges this possibility in a later section of his study: *ibid.*, 90-92.

[35] A. Galmés, "Interés en el orden lingüístico de la literatura española aljamiado-morisca", *Actes Strasbourg*, II, 540-541.

[36] R. Kontzi, *Thesaurus* (*BICC*), XXV (1970), 196-213, esp. 200, 206-207; Galmés, *Batallas*, 9-34.

[37] Alvar claims that "La castellanización (*it* > *ch*) se cumple... con total predominio desde 1480-1481" (*Dial.*, 164); but the *nwey*(*te*) and *feyto* of our MSS prove that Castilianization had still not overtaken the Moriscos in the following century.

[38] See C. López-Morillas, "Trilingual Marginal Notes (Arabic, Aljamiado, and Spanish) in a Morisco Manuscript from Toledo", forthcoming in *JAOS*.

[39] Alvar gives a date of 1518 for the regular occurrence of *h* for *f* in Aragonese documents (*Dial.*, 164); but we cannot reasonably assume that the four MSS in which F- predominates (BN 5078, BN 4938, P 425, and J 25) all predate 1518, since Aljamiado texts from the late fifteenth and very early sixteenth centuries are rare. Again Alvar has not considered the peculiar archaism of Aljamiado (cf. note 37, above).

III. Tafsīr.

Tafsīr, or Qur'ānic exegesis, has been called "the fundamental Muslim science" [1]. "Fundamental" here may refer either to chronological primacy —since some kind of interpretation of the Qur'ān was practised virtually in the Prophet's own time— or to the relationship of exegesis not only to religious thought in Islam but to almost every branch of intellectual endeavor: *ḥadīth* or tradition, history, law, grammar and philology. For many centuries, the best minds in Islam brought their powers to bear on the annotating, interpreting, and clarification of the book they believed to be the sum total of God's revealed word to man. The result has been an enormous body of exegetical literature which remains today at the very center of Islamic religious studies.

The Qur'ān is a work singularly in need of interpretation. Like the Bible, it contains many passages of straightforward historical narrative or legal exposition. But at the same time it employs, to a much higher degree than the Jewish or Christian scriptures, a hermetic and allusive language which inspires and exhorts more than it explains —a language which even, to the non-Muslim ear, seems to sacrifice meaning to sound, logic to rhyme. For the unschooled believer, the rhythmic, musical, and incantatory properties of Qur'ānic prose must provide a large part of the emotional satisfaction of his faith. But the theologian who addresses himself to a serious Muslim audience needs to probe below this glittering surface in order to shed light on obscurities, to expand ideas concentrated into a minimum of words, to disentangle complexities of grammar. Thus from the very beginning Islamic culture fostered the specialized branch of learning called *tafsīr,* devoted to making the meaning of the divine message accessible to all believers.

The first *mufassir* or Qur'ān commentator was Muḥammad's own cousin, ᶜAbd Allah ibn ᶜAbbās (d. 687-88); an extant *tafsīr* is attributed to him, and he was considered an authority on his subject [2]. But the genre did not come to its full flowering until the Middle Ages. By then, the greatest scholars were able to draw on several centuries of accumulated tradition regarding Muḥammad's life and sayings, much of which illuminated obscure passages of the divine revelation. Successive layers of Qur'ānic exegesis, by which later writers incorporated and revised the interpretations of their predecessors, led to the compiling of monumental commentaries that filled tens of volumes. Several of these classic works of *tafsīr* remain the basis for contemporary Qur'ān interpretation and are of significance for the present study; herewith a brief sketch, in chronological order, of the authors and their works.

Aṭ-Ṭabarī, *Jāmiᶜ al-bayān fī tafsīr al-Qur'ān* [3]. Ṭabarī (839?-923 A. D.), one of Islām's greatest historians, brings together in his commentary masses of earlier accounts and traditions, often conflicting. A characteristic of his method is to set down all previous opinions relating to a given passage, and to conclude by revealing which, if any, he finds satisfactory, and why. His work, because of its encyclopaedic nature, has remained a mine of information for later scholars [4]. (It is now acknowledged, however, that most of the sayings attributed to the Prophet that are incorporated into *tafsīr* are spurious, having been invented well after Muḥammad's lifetime [5].)

Az-Zamakhsharī, *Al-Kashshāf ᶜan ḥaqā'iq at-tanzīl* [6]. This Persian *mufassir* (1075-1144) reveals in his work his Muᶜtazilite or free-thinking views, but his *Kashshāf* has nonetheless been widely read by the orthodox. Unlike Ṭabarī, he pays little attention to tradition, concentrating on dogmatic and philosophical questions as well as on rhetoric and lexicography [7].

Fakhr ad-Dīn ar-Rāzī, *Mafātīḥ al-ghaib,* popularly known as *at-Tafsīr al-kabīr* or "the great *tafsīr*" [8]. Rāzī (d. 1209-1210) comments as exhaustively as Ṭabarī, but without quoting chains of traditions as does the latter. Rather, his technique consists of disassembling every concept into its smallest components, each of which is then subjected to close logical and linguistic analysis. He is judicious in evaluating the opinions of others and in offering his own conclusions.

Al-Bayḍāwī, *Anwār at-tanzīl wa-asrār at-ta'wīl* [9]. The *tafsīr* of Bayḍāwī (d. 1286 or 1293) was conceived as a challenge to that of Zamakhsharī, and refutes or suppresses most of the latter's Muᶜtazilite views in order to make the work acceptable to orthodox Islam. The *Anwār* has proved extremely popular, has itself been the subject of later commentaries, and is often taught in the schools. It is distinguished, like other of the author's works, by its extreme conciseness [10].

Muslim Spain, though geographically removed from the center of Islam, was by no means isolated from its intellectual currents; and al-Andalus, while aware of the classic works of *tafsīr* just described, also produced its own interpreters of the Qur'ān. Some or all of the commentaries of the following four have survived:

Ibn Abī Zamanīn, *Tafsīr al-Qur'ān.* This Mālikite jurist from Elvira (936-1008) summarized the commentary of his predecessor, Yaḥyā ibn Salām al-Baṣrī, a North African (d. 815). A fragment consisting of the first six Qur'ānic Sūras exists in three different MS versions, one of them in Aljamiado [11]; the latter represents, in fact, the only extant example of any *tafsīr* that was unquestionably known to the Moriscos [12].

Ibn ᶜAṭiyya al-Gharnāṭi, *Al-muḥarrar al-wajīz fī tafsīr al-kitāb al-ᶜazīz.* Ibn ᶜAṭiyya (1088-1151) spent his entire career in Spain, holding various important posts including that of *qāḍī* of Almería [13]. His commentary was praised both by Ibn Khaldūn, who claimed that it was the first *tafsīr* to scrutinize critically the traditions it contained (*Muqaddima,* II, 446), and by Ibn Taimiyya (*Itqān,* II, 178) [14], as well as by two later *mufassirūn* from Spain, al-Qurṭubī and Abū Ḥayyān (see below) [15]. Particularly striking is the use made of Ibn ᶜAṭiyya's work by Christian polemicists against Islam. When Martín García, bishop of Barcelona (d. 1521), directed a series of sermons to the Moriscos, he drew for his knowledge of Islamic doctrine on materials prepared —apparently from memory— by his canon Juan Andrés, who had served as the *faqīh* of Játiva before his conversion to Christianity. The Qur'ānic exegetes most frequently quoted in the sermons are Zamakhsharī and Ibn ᶜAṭiyya [16]. An edition of *al-Muḥarrar* is in the process of publication, with only one volume produced to date (Cairo, 1974), and another edition has been announced in Morocco [17].

Al-Qurṭubī, *Jāmiᶜ li-ahkām al-qur'ān.* This scholar, born in Cordova as his name implies, died in Upper Egypt in 1273. His *tafsīr* [18] is voluminous, introducing lively anecdotes drawn, in all likelihood, from earlier commentators and from popular tradition.

Abū Ḥayyān al-Gharnāṭī, *Al-baḥr al-muḥīṭ fī tafsīr al-qur'ān.* A member of a Berber family, born in Granada, Abū Ḥayyān became a respected professor of Qur'ānic studies in Cairo, where he died in 1345 [19]. He distinguished himself particularly as a grammarian, and included in his *tafsīr* [20] so much linguistic information that the work was criticized for containing "everything except *tafsīr*".

There remains, in addition to the commentaries of these four scholars, evidence of other works of *tafsīr* circulating in Spain as late as the fifteenth and sixteenth centuries. First we may recall that the Spanish translation of the Qur'ān prepared by ᶜĪsā ibn Jābir in 1456 incorporated passages of commentary drawn from Arabic sources (see Introduction, p. 13). Thus, not only were works of Arabic *tafsīr* available in the *mudéjar* community of Toledo at that late date (nearly four centuries after its reconquest by the Christians), but, if ᶜĪsā's translation enjoyed the currency we have assumed, the Moriscos would have been able to read Qur'ānic exegesis in Spanish or Aljamiado as well. (The implications of this possibility will be discussed further below.) Second, proof of the continuation of ᶜĪsā's influence into the sixteenth century exists in the person and writings of the Mancebo de Arévalo [21]. Three works of this indefatigable Morisco traveler, who lived in the first half of the sixteenth century, survive: the *Breve compendio de nuestra santa ley y suna,* a direct descendant of ᶜĪsā ibn Jābir's *Breviario sunni* or *Kitāb segobiano* of 1462 [22]; *Sumario de la relación y ejercicio espiritual*; and *Tafsira.* The latter term, though suggesting a commentary on the Qur'ān, must have had a broader meaning for the Moriscos, for the work is in fact a general religious treatise or book of devotions [23].

If the Mancebo de Arévalo knew ᶜĪsā's *Breviario,* a collection of extracts and fragments of earlier devotional works, he may well have been acquainted with ᶜĪsā's version of the Qur'ān and its interpolated commentaries. Certainly, his wide reading had brought him into contact with many other works labelled "tafsir(a)", none of which are now identifiable. Many of the titles he cites are suggestive, if puzzling: *el nebuloso tafsir de ᶜUmar Bey, la rubicunda tafsira, el tafsir al-aršikal, el tafsir ebraico, un tafsir rubricado de los logros, un tafsir que trataba de la alfadila de Šaᶜaben, la tafsira de la deballaçión, la primera tafsira de la decretança de los nahues de Almería* [24]. If even a few of these represent genuine interpretations of the Qur'ān, and not merely pious treatises, then the *tafsīr* genre must have continued to flourish in Spain well into the Morisco period.

In the absence of firmer evidence, our best witnesses to knowledge of *tafsīr* among the Moriscos remain the Aljamiado translations of the Qur'ān themselves. These render into Romance not only the scriptural text but more or less extensive commentaries upon it, and these commentaries must be based on Arab authorities. It remains to be determined which exegetes were particularly favored by the translators, and an answer may be found only by comparing the Aljamiado versions in detail with standard works of Arabic *tafsīr.* We will now proceed to such a comparison.

The basis for the exercise is not all forty-six verses of Sūra 79, but two selected passages: verses 1-5 and 15-26. These two portions can, for different reasons, prove particularly useful in revealing their sources. The five opening verses of the Sūra consist of a series of oaths whose language is compressed, hermetic, and of very problematic interpretation. The oaths are couched in the hortatory tone characteristic of the Meccan Sūras, and seem to spring from a vision that was clear to the Prophet at the moment of revelation, but that became obscured in its verbal transmission. Since opinions on the meaning of these verses vary from one exegete to another, it should not be difficult to identify which authority the Aljamiado versions follow.

Verses 15-26 contain a retelling (one of several in the Qur'ān[25]) of part of the story of Moses, a prophet in Islam as in Judaism and Christianity. Here too the tale is told in the briefest and most allusive language possible, so that a good deal of explanation is necessary to flesh out the bare bones of the account. The exegetes supply that elaboration, but each in his own way, so that no two commentaries are alike. A story with such a long history as that of Moses —beginning in the earliest Jewish tradition, and trailing a millenium and a half of existence by Muḥammad's time— attracts variants and re-interpretations. Again, the Aljamiado versions may follow one particular tradition of exegesis in preference to others.

The works of *tafsīr* on which we base this textual comparison are the four principal ones from the East, those of Ṭabarī (*Ṭ*), Zamakhsharī (*Z*), Rāzī (*R*), and Bayḍāwī (*B*), and one from Spain, that of Qurṭubī (*Q*) (the only Spanish *tafsīr* available which contains Sūra 79). Proceeding through the total of seventeen verses in the two passages chosen, we will outline the explanations of each commentary and compare them with those in the Morisco MSS, then summarize what patterns of imitation, if any, emerge.

1: *Wa-n-nāziᶜāti gharqan,* "By those that pluck out vehemently": All five Arab authors offer several possible interpretations, but all put the same one first: that the "pluckers" are the angels who seize the souls of unbelievers after their death. Alternative explanations for *an-nāziᶜāt* are the souls themselves (*Ṭ, R, B, Q*); death (*Ṭ, Q*); bows (*Ṭ, Q*); horses (*Z, B*); and hands of warriors (*Z, Q*). Aside from angels, the only other possibility on which all five agree is stars, and *B* specifies stars which are drawn from the East to the West (*R* speaks, somewhat less precisely, of stars drawn from one side of the earth to the other). All the Morisco versions agree with Bayḍāwī, e. g., P 425: *laš eštrellaš ke parten de šallyente i še funden en ponyente.*

2: *Wa-n-nāshiṭāti nashṭan,* "and those that draw out violently": *Z, B,* and *Q* affirm that these beings are the same as those referred to in verse 1 (i. e., angels *or* stars *or* souls, etc.). All five favor angels as the most likely interpretation; other suggestions are death (*Ṭ*), stars (*Ṭ, R*), nooses (*Ṭ*), wild cows (*Ṭ*), horses (*Z*), and souls (*R*). The Arab commentators all agree that the important factor is the manner of the action: while, in verse 1, it was a violent pulling, here it is a gentle one: the *nāshiṭāt,* if in fact they are angels, draw out the souls of the believers softly and painlessly. The Morisco translators are unanimous in favoring angels (*por loš almalakeš*), but all employ the verb *arrancar*, which suggests the opposite of gentleness. In this respect they remain closer to the Qur'ān itself than to the fine distinction drawn by the *mufassirūn.*

3: *Wa-s-sābiḥāti sabḥan,* "by those that swim serenely": These swimmers suggest to the commentators all manner of possibilities. Again, they may be angels, since these descend to earth as if swimming (*Ṭ, R*), swim in carrying out God's orders (*Z*), pull out souls gently like one swimming in the sea (*R, Q*), resemble divers bringing up something from the bottom of the sea (*B*), or never cease swimming because God's greatness is unceasing (*R*). Otherwise, the *sābiḥāt* may be death, because it swims in men's souls (*Ṭ, Q*); swift horses (*R, Q*); warriors, who hasten to fight as if swimming (*B*); stars, which seem to swim in the sky (*Ṭ, Z, R, Q*); or the souls of the believers that "swim" toward God (*Q*). Only *Ṭ* and *Q* offer the interpretation of ships, the latter specifying ships that swim in the sea. All the Spanish translations follow Qurṭubī, e. g., J 25, *loš bašilloš ke andan por la mar*.

4: *Fa-s-sābiqāti sabqan,* "and those that outstrip suddenly": All five Arab writers prefer to see these figures as angels. Most also stress the idea of haste: the angels hasten in obeying orders (*Z, R*), or in taking the souls of the dead to heaven or hell (*R, B, Q*). Further, they outdo men in belief, obedience (*R*), and good works (*Q*), and they outstrip devils in gaining the ear of prophets (*R, Q*). Besides angels, all the other creatures suggested by the term *sābiqāt* share the quality of speed or swiftness. There is death, because it overtakes man (*Ṭ, Q*); horses (*Ṭ, Z*), because they rush to meet the enemy (*B*) in holy war (*Q*); stars that move in their courses (*Ṭ, Z, B*), some overtaking others (*Q*); warriors who hasten to fight (*B*); and finally the souls of men (*B*), because these outstrip bodies in arriving in heaven or hell (*Q*). In the Aljamiado versions there is universal agreement on interpreting *sābiqāt* as angels: BN 4938, *loš almalakeš ke še abansaron en la obidensya de Allah.* The MSS follow most closely Zamakhsharī and Rāzī, both of whom explicitly mention the angels' haste in obeying God's orders.

5: *Fa-l-muddabirāti amran,* "by those that direct an affair": Once again, these "directors" are perceived as angels by all the Arab exegetes. The angels carry out God's orders (*Ṭ, R*), manage the affairs of His servants (*Z*), order the matter of punishment or reward (*B*), and reveal and allot what is permitted (*ḥalāl*) and what is forbidden (*ḥarām*) (*Q*). They control the earth by regulating the wind and rain (*Q*); and they may belong to the category of archangels (*R, Q*). Still, there remain other interpretations of *muddabirāt*: as horses (*Z, B*); as stars, which determine mathematics (*Z*), the times and seasons and the hours of worship (*B*), and (specifically the Pleiades) the movement of the earth (*Q*); and as souls (*B*). All the Morisco texts choose to see the "directors" as angels. All, likewise, follow Ṭabarī and Rāzī in highlighting the angels' role in carrying out orders from God (e. g., BN 5078, *rriğe Allah kon elloš lo ke kyere*). T 235 adds nothing further, but the MSS written in Aljamiado specify, like Qurṭubī, that it is the angels' task to convey what is permitted or forbidden: BN 4938, *bašan kon la determinasyon de lo halāl y de lo harām.*

Both *R* and *B* conclude their analyses of these first verses of Sūra 79 by affirming that all five refer to the same thing: that is, that the *nāziʿāt, nāshiṭāt, sābiḥāt,* etc. are either all angels, or all stars, or all souls, and that the Qur'ān simply varies the language used to express the concept. The Morisco translators obviously do not share this perception of homogeneity, since they agree on the various interpretations stars, angels, ships, angels, and angels, respectively. More important to note is that the Morisco versions inevitably agree among themselves on one given interpretation for each verse. We will return eventually to the significance of this fact.

15: *Hal atāka ḥadīth Mūsā,* "Hast thou received the story of Moses?": There is no significant commentary on this verse.

16: *Idhā nādāhu rabbuhu bi-l-wādi l-muqaddasi Ṭuwā,* "When his Lord called to him in the holy valley, Towa": *B* remarks that *Sūrat Ṭaha* (Sūra 20, which contains an extensive account of the Moses legend) clarifies this verse.

17: *Idhhab ilā Firʿawna innahu ṭaghā,* "Go to Pharaoh; he has waxed insolent": *Ṭ* and *Q* explain that these words were spoken by God to Moses; following them, four Aljamiado translations (BN 5078, P 425, J 39, J 25) insert the words *Dišo Allah a Mūsā,* and the other two add more briefly *I dišole Allah* (BN 4938) or *Y le dixo* (T 235). *R* refers the reader to *Sūrat Ṭaha* for an account of how Moses was to understand God's command. For the verb *ṭaghā, Ṭ* and *Q* give the meaning 'to exceed the limit in pride or rebellion against God'. According to *R, ṭaghā* implies that Pharaoh disbelieved in his Creator when he insisted that his people serve him as their Lord. The six Morisco texts agree here with Rāzī, employing the terms *a deškre(y)ido* or *desconoçe.*

18: *Fa-qul hal laka ilā an tazakkā,* "And say, 'Hast thou the will to purify thyself'": All the Arab commentators focus here on the sense of the verb *tazakkā.* Most feel that it means 'to be purified': from unbelief (*Ṭ, B*), from polytheism (*Z*), or from sin (*Q*). Other possible meanings are 'to submit (to God's will)', as a synonym for *aslama* (*Ṭ, Q*); or 'to recite the profession of faith, "There is no god but God"' (*T, Q*). *R* maintains that *tazakkā* consists simply of believing in God, leading a proper life, and keeping the laws of the faith. Of the Morisco versions, J 25 reproduces faithfully the words of Ṭabarī and Bayḍāwī: *a ke te alinpyeš de la deškreyensya.* In the other five MSS, the exhortation to believe in God (*ke kreaš en/kon Allah*) is closest in spirit to Rāzī's interpretation.

19: *Wa-ahdīka ilā rabbika fa-takhshā,* "And that I should guide thee to thy Lord, then thou shalt fear": *Ṭ* explains that these are the words God wishes Moses to address to Pharaoh. The first three words of the verse, according to *R,* stress the importance of obedience to God, and *Q* interprets them more precisely as meaning, "I will take you to obedience of your Lord". BN 4938 thus follows Qurṭubī: *yo te gío a la obidensya de tu šennor.* All the other translations substitute for "obedience" the Arabic term *ad(d)īn,* 'religion'. All the Arab exegetes seek also to convey exact nuances of the term *takhshā. Q* calls it simply 'fear'. *Ṭ* considers it fear of punishment for not doing God's will, or for rebelling; otherwise, it may be the fear which comes from knowledge (*Z*), specifically knowledge of God (*B*). *R* reverses the terms: one fears God in order to know Him. None of the six translations elaborates on what kind of fear is represented by [*aber*]*myedo* or [*temer*]; in their economy of expression they most closely approximate Qurṭubī.

20: *Fa-arāhu l-āyata l-kubrā,* "So he showed him the great sign": The Arabic word *āya* means both 'sign' and 'miracle'; the reference here is to the miracle God performed before Moses, recounted at greater length in *Sūrat Ṭaha,* as *R* points out. In that chapter (as in the Old Testament account in Exodus 4:1-7) there are actually two miracles: Moses' staff changes into a snake and back again, and his hand turns white on being thrust into his bosom, then is restored. *B* mentions only the miracle of the staff. For the other four *mufassirūn,* the "great sign" may mean either the staff or the hand, or both (*Ṭ, Z, Q*); *R* inclines to believe that the miracle of the staff is greater, since that object changes its nature while the hand alters only in color. *Q* adds that the "great sign" might also refer to the parting of the Red Sea, or even indicate the sum total of all God's miracles. None of the Morisco versions mentions Moses' staff at all in connection with this verse. T 235, here as elsewhere the least prolix of the MSS, adds no commentary to the bare translation of the Qur'ān's words. The five Aljamiado MSS explain the miracle of the hand in varying degrees of detail: J 25 is content with a brief reference (*el milagro mayor de šu mano rrelunbrante*); BN 5078, P 425 and J 39 all are more specific about the process of the miracle (e. g., BN 5078, *šu mano ke la šakaba de šu šeno blanka rrelunbrante*); and BN 4938 dwells at considerable length on the appearance of the hand during its transformation and restoration (*tan rrelunbrante komo una pyedra kreštal ... depweš ... šakabala komo š-era de anteš de karne i de gwešo*). In not speaking of the miracle of the staff, the Morisco versions do not seem to descend from any of our five Arabic commentaries; nor do the latter refer to Moses' total of nine miracles, of which BN 5078, P 425, J 39, and BN 4938 all make a particular point. The translations must be following here one or more works of *tafsīr* of which we are unaware; perhaps these referred to Sūra 27: 12, which speaks of the nine signs that God showed to Pharaoh.

21: *Fa-kadhdhaba wa-ᶜaṣā,* "But he cried lies, and rebelled": The Arabic commentaries are all in substantial agreement on this verse. Pharaoh disbelieved (*Ṭ, Z, Q*) or denied (*R*) Moses' miracle and its message, and consequently disobeyed Moses' command (*Ṭ*), thus rebelling against God (*Z, Q*) out of pride (*R*). The Morisco translators are unanimous in their choice of the verbs *(d)ešmintyo* and *dešobedesyo*; it would be difficult to claim that they follow one commentator rather than another.

22: *Thumma adbara yasᶜā,* "Then he turned away hastily": The various *tafsīrs* seek to establish what Pharaoh turned away from, and why. The turning could be a rejection of Moses and his message (*Ṭ, R*), or, more seriously, a sign of rebellion against God (*Ṭ, B*) or shunning of belief (*Q*). *Z, R, B* and *Q* also suggest that Pharaoh turned in fear of the snake that Moses' staff had become, and this opinion is the only one taken up by the five Aljamiado MSS (T 235, again, omits all commentary). (Note that the MSS are introducing the staff and snake for the first time, not having mentioned them in connection with verse 20.) All agree that Pharaoh turned back hastily, fleeing from the snake (BN 4938, *tornoše rredra saga kon afollamyento i fuyendo de la kulwebra*). In language they most closely resemble Qurṭubī's *tafsīr,* the only one to speak specifically of "escaping".

23: *Fa-ḥashara fa-nādā,* "Then he mustered and proclaimed": Pharaoh gathered his people (*Ṭ, Z, R, Q*) or his army (*B, Q*). All the Morisco versions agree on "people" (*ǧent*[*e*]).

24: *Fa-qāla anā rabbukum al-aᶜlā,* "And he said, 'I am your Lord, the Most High'": *Ṭ,* after quoting Pharaoh's blasphemous words, adds *wa-kadhdhaba l-aḥmaq* 'and the foolish one lied', a sentiment echoed exactly by BN 4938's *šalboše Allah, ke akello era mintira. Q* clarifies that *anā rabbukum ...* means, "you have no other lord but me". The other exegetes defer their remarks on this significant phrase to their discussion of verse 25, and the Morisco MSS other than BN 4938 add no commentary.

25: *Fa-ākhadhahu-llahu nakāla l-ākhirati wa-l-ūlā,* "So God seized him with the chastisement of the Last World and the First": The Arabic commentaries speculate at great length upon the nature of the two punishments that God visited on Pharaoh. Pharaoh may have been chastised for his two blasphemous statements: first, "I have shown you no other god but me", and second, "I am your Lord the Most High" (*Ṭ, Z, R, B, Q*). Forty years elapsed between the two utterances (*Ṭ, Z, R, Q*); God overlooked the first one out of forgiveness, but punished Pharaoh after the second (*R, Q*). Alternatively, God may have punished the blasphemer twice, in this world and in the next (*Ṭ, Z, R, B, Q*); the punishment in this life was drowning (*R, B, Q*) —or drowning in pain (*Ṭ*)—, and in the other life, burning (*B*). Other interpretations which the commentators offer, but seem to consider less likely, are that God punished Pharaoh at both the beginning and the end of his wicked action (*Ṭ*) or of his life (*Q*); that the "first" represents Pharaoh's disbelief in God (*Ṭ*) or in Moses and his miracles (*R, Q*), with the "last" then meaning his statement "I am your Lord" (*Ṭ, R, Q*). *Nakāl* may be taken to mean either 'strong pain' (*R*), or 'an exemplary punishment, one that restrains others from sin' (*R, Q*). The Morisco translations simplify considerably this wealth of possibilities. None mentions Pharaoh's two sacrilegious pronouncements nor the supposed forty years between them. All, on the other hand, agree with one opinion of the five *tafsīrs* that the two punishments are those of the present world and the next; all but T 235 mention that God drowned Pharaoh, thus agreeing with Rāzī, Bayḍāwī, and Qurṭubī. The Aljamiado versions, however, add to the Arabic the words *en la mar* 'in the sea' —presumably the Red Sea, during Pharaoh's pursuit of the children of Israel. There is thus no close correlation between the Morisco versions and any single Arabic *tafsīr*; the former must all be following here some other commentator who summarized simply that Pharaoh was punished in the other world, and in this one by drowning in the sea.

26: *Inna fī dhālika la-ᶜibratan li-man yakhshā,* "Surely in that is a lesson for him who fears": *B* and *Q* merely paraphrase the verse. *R* does substantially the same, though at greater length, adding that the warning is directed to those who fear that God will visit upon them the same punishment that He dealt to Pharaoh. The phrase common to the five Aljamiado MSS, e. g., P 425, *ke no le akaeska šenblante de lo ke akaesyo a Firᶜawn,* thus resembles Rāzī's interpretation, though the words are not a direct translation of his.

Now that we have made the detailed comparison between the five Qur'ān commentaries in Arabic and the six Morisco MSS, what conclusions can we draw? The one unequivocal fact that emerges is that there is no consistent correspondence between the Morisco versions (singly or collectively) and any given Arabic *tafsīr*. One or more of the MSS from Spain approximates, at a rough count, Ṭabarī eight times, Zamakhsharī six, Rāzī ten, Bayḍāwī six, and Qurṭubī nine, in the course of these seventeen verses. But there is no clear preference for the interpretation of one individual exegete; and in two or three verses the Morisco translators do not seem to be considering any of these Arab authorities.

On the other hand, there exists a notable similarity among the Morisco versions themselves in the wording of their interpolated commentaries. For the first five verses of the Sūra, in the face of the multiplicity of interpretations offered by the standard *tafsīrs,* the readings of the MSS are virtually identical. The texts could hardly have achieved such unanimity had each Morisco scribe adopted the view of a favorite commentator. For verses 15-26, although the Spanish versions vary somewhat more, there remains all the same an overwhelming impression of mutual resemblance. Only T 235, in both groups of verses, stands slightly apart. In verses 2-5, it attempts a literal translation of the Arabic (*por los arrancantes arrancamiento,* etc.) before adding the explanatory phrase. During the Moses episode, this Toledo MS generally shuns all commentary and limits itself to rendering the words of the Qur'ān only. We have already speculated that T 235 represents a translation of the Qur'ān entirely separate from the others (see Introduction); and its independence in the handling of *tafsīr* material confirms that supposition.

Even setting T 235 aside, we are left with five Aljamiado MSS which all interpret the Qur'ān in the same way and with practically the same words, yet do not follow consistently any of the major Arabic commentaries. The inescapable conclusion is that they derive from a common model now lost to us, a translation of the Qur'ān whose author had consulted a variety of Arabic *tafsīrs,* digested and summarized them, and incorporated into his version what he considered to be the most reasonable and useful opinions. The resulting translation-plus-commentary would have circulated as a widely accepted standard, frequently copied and consulted, especially as a knowledge of Arabic sufficient to read the original *tafsīr* faded among the Moriscos. The standard version presumably was elastic and permitted variation, and could be altered by a copyist with the ability to do so: BN 4938, for example, shows more extensive interpolations than the other MSS, and its translator may have consulted other Arabic or Spanish commentaries on his own.

This assumption of a standard Aljamiado translation of the Qur'ān will by now sound familiar to the reader: we had already surmised its existence at the end of the Introduction, after comparing the readings of the various Aljamiado MSS. And once again we suggest that the author who combed the Arabic authorities for their interpretations and condensed the results into a simplified running commentary was none other than ᶜĪsā ibn Jābir. We know that his lost Spanish translation included selected passages of commentary; we have speculated that his reputation assured the general adoption of his version of the Qur'ān. Thus it is likely that ᶜĪsā, rather than Zamakhsharī, Qurṭubī, or Abu Ḥayyān, became in effect the chief interpreter of the Qur'ān to the Moriscos.

NOTES.

1 A. J. Arberry, *Sufism* (London, 1950), 70.

2 *EI,* IV, 603-604.

3 Ed. Būlāq, 1323-30 A. H. (=1905-12 A. D.), 30 vols. The commentary on Sūra 79 is in Vol. 30, 18-32.

4 *EI,* IV, 578-579.

5 *Ibid.,* IV, 604.

6 Ed. Cairo, 1948, 3 vols. Sūra 79 in Vol. 3, 308-312.

7 *EI,* IV, 1205-1207.

8 Ed. at-Tizām ᶜAbd ar-Raḥmān Muḥammad (Cairo, 1934), 32 vols. Sūra 79 in Vol. 31, 27-53.

9 Ed. Cairo, 1330 A. H. (=1911-12 A. D.), 4 vols. Sūra 79 in Vol. 4, 171-173.

10 *EI* (new ed.), I, 1129.

11 *GAL,* I, 205; the MSS are J 51 (Escuela de Estudios Arabes, Madrid), in Aljamiado; No. 34, al-Qarawiyyīn, Fez, in Arabic; and no. 820, British Museum, in Arabic (I have been unable to consult T. Losada Campo's Barcelona dissertation, *Estudios sobre coranes aljamiados* [1975], based on all three MSS).

12 L. P. Harvey, *The Literary Culture of the Moriscos 1492-1609. A Study Based on the Extant MSS in Arabic and Aljamía,* unpublished D. Phil. dissertation (Magdalen College, Oxford, 1958), 145.

13 *GAL,* I, 525.

14 R. J. Ahmad, *IQ,* XII (1968), 85.

15 J. Vernet, *StIsl,* XXXII (1970), 305-309.

16 *Ibid.,* 305-306; and J. Vernet, *Actas,* 137-140.

17 A. A. ᶜAbd al-Barr, *Daᶜwat al-Haqq,* XII: 4 (1388/1969), 57-71. Vernet (*Actas,* 143, n. 26) speaks of a fragment of Ibn ᶜAṭiyya's *tafsīr* (Sūras 5-7) in the Ateneo library of Barcelona; but, having been copied in 1216/1801-02, it would not have been available to the Moriscos.

18 Ed. Cairo, 1967, 19 vols. Sūra 79 in Vol. 19, 190-210. See also *GAL,* I, 529.

19 *GAL,* II, 133. See also *EI* (new ed.), I, 126; and F. Pons Boigues, *Ensayo bio-bibliográfico sobre los historiadores y geógrafos españoles* (Madrid, 1898), 323-326.

20 Ed. Cairo, 1328 A. H. (=1910-11 A. D.), 8 vols. Unavailable for consultation.

21 See L. P. Harvey, *And,* XXIII (1958), 49-74; *MPh,* LXV (1967-68), 130-132; *Actas,* 21-42.

22 Harvey, *Actas,* 35-36.

23 *Ibid.,* 27.

24 *Ibid.,* 34.

25 See, in addition to Sūra 79, Sūras 7, 20, 26, 27, and 28.

IV. The texts.

The forty-six verses of Sūra 79 have been arranged as follows: the number of the verse (an italic Arabic numeral) appears at the upper left-hand corner. Heading the page is the verse in Arabic, followed by an English translation. (The English version is that of A. J. Arberry, *The Koran Interpreted* [London, 1955]; while not strictly literal, it is widely admired as having captured to a great degree the sense and rhythm of the original.) There follow the six Morisco versions of the verse, in this order: BN 5078, P 425, J 39, J 25, BN 4938, and T 235 (note that J 39 lacks verses 1-5, while BN 5078 lacks 41-46). This order of the MSS is not chronological (for their relative chronology see above, pp. 42-45), but rather groups the different versions according to their similarities and possible affiliations. Thus BN 5078 and P 425, assumed to be copies of a common original, are placed together; the two J MSS, whose wording resembles in some cases that of the first two, but which do not seem to form part of the same stemma, follow (J 39 preceding because of its somewhat closer resemblance to P 425). BN 4938 and T 235 each, apparently, represents an independent tradition; the latter is placed last to emphasize its unique character as the only MS written in Latin script.

Square brackets used alone enclose material omitted by the scribe. Brackets accompanied by a footnote contain material lost through later deterioration of the MS, blurring of the photograph, etc. Critical emendations are also indicated in the footnotes. T 235 makes occasional use of two abbreviations, "q" and "vro(s)", which have been expanded as q*ue* and v*uest*ro(s), respectively.

For the system of transliteration of the Aljamiado versions see above, pp. 27-29. It may be assumed that, in syllable-initial consonant clusters, the vowel omitted is homorganic with the following vowel, e. g. *tenbalanteš* appears as *tenblanteš, eškubiriršc* as *eškubriršc*; any exceptions to this rule are recorded in the footnotes.

Words are separated wherever all their elements are present in the Arabic script, e. g. أَنْ اَلْ = *en el*. In cases of elision the words are linked by a hyphen, e. g. *š-entyende, d-ella.*

The dotted *y* (*ẏ*) which appears occasionally in T 235 does not seem to be significant (it does not distinguish a vocalic from a consonantal sound), so the dot has been omitted in transcription.

Punctuation has been added; accent marks are used sparingly, only where they are needed to clarify meaning.

وَٱلنَّازِعَاتِ غَرْقًا

1

By those that pluck out vehemently

BN 5078: E ğuró Allah por laš eštrellaš ke še parten del šallyent e še funden en el ponyent;

P 425: Ğuró Allah por laš eštrellaš ke parten de šallyente i še funden en ponyente;

J 39:

J 25: Ğuró Allah por laš eštrellaš ke parten de šallyente i še funden en el ponyente;

BN 4938: Ğuró Allah por laš eštrellaš ke parten del šallyent i še ponen i še funden en el ponyent;

T 235: Juró Allah por la[s] estrellas que parten del saliente y se funden en el poniente;

وَٱلنَّاشِطَاتِ نَشْطًا

2

and those that draw out violently,

BN 5078: i por loš almalakeš ke arranka[n] [1] loš arruḥeš de loš kreyenteš;

P 425: i por loš almalakeš ke arrankan loš arruḥeš de loš kreyenteš;

J 39:

J 25: i por loš almalakeš ke arrankan loš arruheš de loš kreyenteš arrankamyento;

BN 4938: i por loš almalakeš ke arrankan loš arruḥeš i ešmenoran loš gwešoš;

T 235: y por los arrancantes arrancamiento, y por los almalaques q*ue* arrancan los arrohes de los creyentes;

---

[1] End of line missing in MS.

وَالسَّابِحَاتِ سَبْحًا

3

by those that swim serenely

BN 5078: i por loš bašyelloš ke andan por la mar;

P 425: i por loš bašilloš ke andan por la mar;

J 39:

J 25: i por loš bašilloš ke andan por la mar;

BN 4938: i por loš bašyelloš ke andan por la mar;

T 235: y por los andantes andamiento, y por los vaxillos q*ue* andan por el mar;

فَالسَّابِقَاتِ سَبْقًا

4

and those that outstrip suddenly

BN 5078: i por loš almalakeš ke še adebantor[o]n en la obedensya de Allah;

P 425: i por loš almalakeš ke še debantaron en la obede[ns]ya [1] d-Allah;

J 39:

J 25: i por loš almalakeš ke še adelantaron en la obidensya de Allah adelantamyento;

BN 4938: i por loš almalakeš ke še abansaron en la obidensya de Allah;

T 235: y por los adelantantes adelantamiento, y por los almalaques q*ue* se adelantaron en la obidiençia de Allah;

---

1 MS blurred.

فَالْمُدَبِّرَاتِ أَمْرًا

5

by those that direct an affair!

BN 5078: i por loš almalakeš ke bašan[1] kon lo ḥalāl i lo ḥarām i rriğe Allah kon elloš lo ke kyere:

P 425: i por loš almalakeš ke bašan kon lo ḥalāl i lo haram i rriğe Allah kon elloš lo ke kyere:

J 39:

J 25: i por loš almalakeš ke bašan kon lo ḥalāl i lo ḥaram i rriğe Allah kon elloš lo ke kyere:

BN 4938: i por loš [almalakeš][2] ke bašan kon la determinasyon de lo halāl i de lo harām i rriğe Allah subḥānahu kon elloš lo ke kyere i ordena lo ke le plaze:

T 235: y por los rregidores en mandamiento, y por los almalaques q*ue* rrige Allah con ellos lo que quiere:

[1] MS: pašan.
[2] Corner of MS page missing.

يَوْمَ تَرْجُفُ الرَّاجِفَةُ

6

Upon the day when the first blast shivers

BN 5078: el dia ke še tokará en la bozina la primera tokada,

P 425: el dia ke še tokará la bozina la primera tokada,

J 39: el dia ke še tokará en la bozina la p[rime]r[a] to[k]ada[1],

J 25: el dia ke še tokará la bozina,

BN 4938: k-el dia ke še tokará el kwerno de Isrāfīl el primero tokido,

T 235: el dia que rretronarán los rretronidos de la vozina,

[1] MS torn.

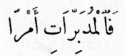

تَتْبَعُهَا ٱلرَّادِفَةُ

7

and the second blast follows it,

BN 5078: i apreš d-ella šera la šegund[a] —i entre la un tokamyento i la otro abrá kwaranta annoš—

P 425: apreš d-ella šera la šegunda —y-entre un tokamyento abrá kwarenta annoš—

J 39: depweš d-ella še šigira la šegunda tokada —y-entre el un tokamyento y-el otro abrá kwarenta annoš—

J 25: i apreš d-ella še šegira la šegunda tokada,

BN 4938: i apreš še rretornará la šegunda tokada —i entre ell un tokido i ell otro kwaranta annoš—

T 235: y seguira tras dellos la voz rretiemblante,

قُلُوبٌ يَوْمَئِذٍ وَاجِفَةٌ

8

hearts upon that day shall be athrob

BN 5078: abrá korasoneš en akel dia tinblanteš[1].

P 425: i abrá korasoneš en akel dia tenblanteš,

J 39: abrá korasoneš akel dia tenblanteš,

J 25: abrá korasoneš akel dia tinblanteš,

BN 4938: en akel dia abrá korasoneš tremulanteš de myedo de Allah,

T 235: abrá corazones aquel dia esbuludreando,

---

[1] MS: tinbelanteš.

أَبْصَارُهَا خَاشِعَةٌ

9

and their eyes shall be humbled.

BN 5078: i loš welloš de akelloš šeran umileš enklinadoš.

P 425: de akelloš šeran umileš en[k]linadoš.

J 39: i šuš bištaš temerošaš enklinadaš.

J 25: i šuš bištaš temerošaš kon umildansa.

BN 4938: i loš oǧoš de akelloš amedresidoš.

T 235: y sus vistas humilladas.

يَقُولُونَ ءَإِنَّا لَمَرْدُودُونَ فِى ٱلْحَافِرَةِ

10

They shall say, "What, are we being restored as we were before?

BN 5078: Dizen loš deškreyenteš en el mundo, "I beamoš, ¿aun emoš a šeyer tornadoš ẖaleqadoš nwebament en laš fwešaš,

P 425: Dizen loš deškreyenteš en el mundo, "Ea, beamoš, ¿aun emoš de šer tornadoš ẖaleqadoš nwebamente en laš fwešaš,

J 39: Dizen loš deškreyenteš en el mundo, "I beamoš, ¿aun emoš de šer rrebibkadoš depweš ke šeamoš mwertoš en laš fwešaš,

J 25: I dizen loš deškreyenteš en el mundo, "I beamoš, ¿aun emoš de šer tornadoš a rrebibkar en las fwešaš,

BN 4938: I dizen loš deškreyenteš en ešte mundo, "I beamoš, ¿aun abemoš de šeyer tornadoš a ẖaleqar nwebament en laš fwešaš para el konto,

T 235: Y deçian los descreyentes en el mundo, "¿Como habemos de ser tornados vivos en las fuesas

إِذَا كُنَّا عِظَامًا نَخِرَةً

11

What, when we are bones old and wasted?"

BN 5078: depweš ke šeyamoš gwašoš menudoš podridoš [1]?"

P 425: depweš ke šeamoš gwešoš podridoš?"

J 39: depweš ke šeamoš gwešoš podridoš?"

J 25: depweš ke šeamoš gwešoš podridoš?"

BN 4938: depweš de šeyer gwešoš podridoš?"

T 235: quando seamos huesos menudos?"

[1] MS: podoridoš.

قَالُوا تِلْكَ إِذًا كَرَّةٌ خَاسِرَةٌ

12

They shall say, "That then were a losing return!"

BN 5078: Dizen loš deškreyenteš keryendo dešmentir, "Akel tornamyento [1] šera tornado mintrošo ke no pwede šeye[r]."

P 425: Tornan i dizen loš deškreyenteš ki[šy]endo [2] ešmentir akel tornamyento, "Akella šera tornada mintroša ke no pwede šer."

J 39: Dizen loš deškreyenteš kišyendo dešmentir, "Akel tornamyento šera tornado mintroš ke no pwede šer."

J 25: Dizen, "Akella šera la ora tornada perdida ke no pwede šer."

BN 4938: Torna i dizen maš loš deškreyenteš ešmintyendo akel tornamyento del konto i dizen, "Akella šera tornada mintroša perdida ke no pwede šeyer."

T 235: Dixeron, "Aquella seria tornada de perdiçion."

[1] MS: torbamiyento.
[2] MS blurred.

فَإِنَّمَا هِىَ زَجْرَةٌ وَاحِدَةٌ

13

But it shall be only a single scare.

BN 5078: E dize Allah, "Pweš šabed berdaderament ke no šera šino un tokamyento en la bozina,

P 425: [D]iz[1]-Allah, "Šabed berdaderamente ke no šera šino un tokamyento en la bozina,

J 39: Dize Allah, "Pweš no šera šino un tokamyento šolo en la bozina,

J 25: Dize Allah, "Pweš šabed ke šera un tokamyento šolo ke šera tokado en la bozina,

BN 4938: I dize Allah subḥānahu, "Šabed berdaderament ke no šera šino un tokamyento en la bozina,

T 235: En ella dixo, "A la fe, ella sera vn soflido solo en la vozina,

[1] Initial letter blurred in MS.

فَإِذَا هُمْ بِالسَّاهِرَةِ

14

and behold, they are awakened.

BN 5078: e lwego šeran šobre la kara de la tyerra."

P 425: i lwego šeran šobre la kara de la tyerra."

J 39: i beošloš šobre la kara de la tyerra."

J 25: i beoš todaš laš ǧenteš rrebibkadaš šobre la kara de la tyerra."

BN 4938: i lwego šeran en la tyerra plana a dar el konto", ke š-entyende ke šera en Ṭūri Sīnā.

T 235: y veos los en la cara de la tierra rebibcados."

هَلْ أَتَيٰكَ حَدِيثُ مُوسَىٰ

15

Hast thou received the story of Moses?

BN 5078: ¿Ya te bino el rrekontamyento de Mūsā,

P 425: "Ya te bino el rrekontamyento de Mūsā,

J 39: ¿Ya te bino el rrekontamyento de Mūsā,

J 25: Dize Allah, "¿Ya te bino el rrekontamyento de Mūsā, yā Muḥammad,

BN 4938: Dišo Allah all annabī Muḥammad, "¿Ate plegado el rrekontamyento de Mūsā,

T 235: Dixo, "¿Ya te vino, ye Muhamed, la ystoria de Muçe,

إِذْ نَادَيٰهُ رَبُّهُ بِالْوَادِ الْمُقَدَّسِ طُوًى

16

When his Lord called to him in the holy valley, Towa:

BN 5078: [k]wando[1] lo klamó šu še[nnor] en el bal šanto de Ṭuwā? ašī era šu nonbre.

P 425: kwando lo klamó šu šennor en el bal šanto de Ṭuwā? aši era[2] šu nonbre.

J 39: kwando lo llamó šu šennor en el bal šanto de Ṭuwā? aši era šu nonbre.

J 25: kwando lo klamó šu šennor en el bal šanto de Ṭuwā?"

BN 4938: kw[ando lo kla]mó[3] šu šennor en el bal šanto de Ṭuwā?" ke ašī[4] še kl[am]a akel monte.

T 235: quando lo llamó su señor al bal sancto[5] de Ttogue?"

---

1 MS: blurred letter, followed by *awando*.
2 MS: ere.
3 Lacuna in MS.
4 MS: asī.
5 Possibly *santo*; what looks like the letter *c* is not completely finished.

اذْهَبْ إِلَى فِرْعَوْنَ إِنَّهُ طَغَى

17

"Go to Pharaoh; he has waxed insolent.

BN 5078: Dīšo Allah a Mūsā, "Beš a Fir^cawna, ke a deškreido.

P 425: Dišo Allah a Mūsā, "Beš a Fir^cawn el deškreido.

J 39: Dīššo Allah a Mūsā, "Beš a Fira^cūn, k-el a deškreido.

J 25: I le dīšo Allah a Mūsā, "Beš a Fira^cūn, k-el a deškreido.

BN 4938: I dišole Allah, "Beš a Fir^cawn, ke el a deškreyido.

T 235: Y le dixo, "Ves a Firaon, que el desconoçe.

فَقُلْ هَلْ لَكَ إِلَى أَنْ تَزَكَّى

18

And say, 'Hast thou the will to purify thyself,

BN 5078: I dīle, '¿Ya te a plegado el mandamyento ke kreyaš en Allah,

P 425: I dile, '¿Ya te a p[l]egado el mandamyento ke kreaš en Allah,

J 39: I dīle, '¿Ya te a llegado el mandamyento de tu šennor en ke kreaš kon Allah,

J 25: I dile, '¿E aši te a plegado el mandemyento de tu šennor a ke te alinpyeš de la deškreyensya,

BN 4938: I dile, '¡Yā Fir^cawn! ¿Ya eš[1] a tī en ke kreaš kon Allah,

T 235: Y dile, '¿A tu es en que creas,

[1] MS: Ya eš eš.

وَأَهْدِيَكَ إِلَى رَبِّكَ فَتَخْشَى

19

and that I should guide thee to thy Lord, then thou shalt fear?'"

BN 5078: i gyarte a al addin de tu šennor pweš aw myedo ada Allah?'"

P 425: i gyarte [a] al addīn de tu šennor pweš abe myedo d-Allah?'"

J 39: i gyarte a al addīn de tu šennor pweš teme ada Allah?'"

J 25: i te gyará al addīn de tu šennor pweš teme ada Allah?'"

BN 4938: i ke yo te gío a la obidensya de tu šennor para ke le ayaš myedo?'"

T 235: y te guiará al adin de tu señor para que temas ada Allah?'"

فَأَرَيهُ الْآيَةَ الْكُبْرَى

20

So he showed him the great sign,

BN 5078: I demoštrole[1] el milagro mayor de šu mano, ke la šakaba de šu šeno blanka rrelunbrante[2]; akel fwe uno de nweb milagroš ke fizo Mūsā.

P 425: I demweštrale [el] milagro mayor de šu mano, ke šakaba de šu šeno blanka rrelunbrante; akel fwe uno de loš nwebe milagroš ke fizo Mūsā.

J 39: I dyole a ber el milagro mayor de šu mano, ke la šakaba de šu šeno blanka rrelunbrante; akel fwe uno de nwebe m[i]lagroš ke hizo Mūsā.

J 25: I dyole a ber el milagro mayor de šu mano rrelunbrante.

BN 4938: E demoštrole el miraglo mayor de todoš loš nwebe miragloš ke hizo Mūsā; i ešte mayor era ke ponia Mūsā šu mano en šu šeno i šakabala tan rrelunbrante komo una pyedra kreštal ke rrapan la bišta de loš oğoš; depweš tornabala otra beš i šakabala komo š-era de anteš de karne i de gwešo.

T 235: Y diole a ver el milagro mayor.

---

1 MS: demostorole.
2 MS: rrelunberante.

فَكَذَّبَ وَعَصَى

21

but he cried lies, and rebelled,

BN 5078: Y-ešmintyo Fir^{c}awn al mandamyento de Allah i dešobedesyolo;

P 425: Y-ešmintyo Fir^{c}awn el mandamyento d-Allah i dešobedesyolo;

J 39: Y-ešmintyo Fira^{c}ūn al mandamyento de Allah i dešobedesyolo;

J 25: I dešmintyo el mandamyento de Allah i dešobedesyolo;

BN 4938: I ešmintyo el mandamyento de Allah i dešobedesyo;

T 235: Y desmintio i desobedeçio;

ثُمَّ أَدْبَرَ يَسْعَى

22

then he turned away hastily,

BN 5078: i tornoše rryedra [1] a saga kon afollamyento i fuyendo de la kulebra [2] ke lansó Mūsā.

P 425: i tornoše a saga kon la follamyenta i fuyendo del kulebro ke lansó Mūsā.

J 39: depweš bolbyoše rridra saga kon afollamyento huyendo de la kulebra ke lansó Mūsā.

J 25: depweš bolbyoše [3] rridra saga fuyendo de la qulebra.

BN 4938: i tornoše rredra saga kon afollamyento i fuyendo de la kulebra de Mūsā —ke lansaba Mūsā su gayata i tornabaše un kulebro.

T 235: despues volbio las cuestas y fuese.

---

1 MS: rriyedera.
2 MS: kulebera.
3 MS: polbiyoše.

فَحَشَرَ فَنَادَىٰ

23

then he mustered and proclaimed,

BN 5078: I fizo plegar la ğent,

P 425: I fizo plegar la ğente,

J 39: I hizo llegar la ğente,

J 25: I fizo plegar la ğente,

BN 4938: I fizo plegar Firᶜawn todaš šu ğenteš,

T 235: Y llegó su gente,

فَقَالَ أَنَا رَبُّكُمُ الْأَعْلَىٰ

24

and he said, "I am your Lord, the Most High!"

BN 5078: i dišo, "Yo šo bweštro šennor el maš šobirano."

P 425: i dišo, "Yo š[o] bweštro šennor el maš šobirano."

J 39: i diššo, "Yo šoy bweštro šennor el maš šoberano."

J 25: i kridó i dišo, "Yo šoy bweštro šennor el maš šoberano."

BN 4938: i dišoleš, "Yo šo bweštro šennor el maš alto i šobirano." Šalboše [1] Allah, ke akello era mintira.

T 235: y gritoles i dixo, "Yo soy v*uest*ro señor el soberano."

---

[1] Possibly intending *šalbo šea* (cf. Ar. *ḥāšā-llah* 'God forbid').

25 فَأَخَذَهُ ٱللَّهُ نَكَالَ ٱلْآخِرَةِ وَٱلْأُولَىٰ

So God seized him with the chastisement of the Last World and the First.

BN 5078: I konprišolo Allah kon la pena del otro mundo i de akešte[1] kwando lo afogó en la mar;

P 425: I konprišolo Allah kon la pena del otro mundo i de akešte kwando lo afogó en la mar;

J 39: I konprendyolo Allah kon la pena de la otra bida i de akešta kwando lo ahogó en la mar i dešanparolo;

J 25: I konprendyolo Allah kon la pena del otro mundo i de akešte, ke lo afogó en la mar;

BN 4938: I konprendyolo Allah kon el krebanso i pena dell otro mundo i d-ešte mundo kwando lo afogó en la mar;

T 235: I comprehendiolo Allah con el tormento de la otra vida y deste mundo;

[1] MS: akešta.

26 إِنَّ فِى ذَٰلِكَ لَعِبْرَةً لِّمَن يَخْشَىٰ

Surely in that is a lesson for him who fears!

BN 5078: ešte eš dešenplo[1] a kyen abrá myedo i temera. ¡Ke no le akaeska[2] šenblante[3] de lo ke akaesyo a Fir^{c}awn i a šu ğent!

P 425: en akello ay inšyenplo a kyen abrá myedo. ¡Ke no le akaeska šenblante de lo ke akaesyo a Fir^{c}awn i a šu ğente!

J 39: en akello ay deššenplo para kyen abrá myedo i temera. ¡Ke no le akaeska šenblante de lo ke akaesyo a Fira^{c}ūn i a šu ğente!

J 25: ke en akello ay dešenplo para kyen teme ada Allah.

BN 4938: kar en akello ay enšenplo para kyen abrá myedo i temor. ¡Ke no le akaeska šemeğante de lo ke akaesyo a Fir^{c}awn!

T 235: q*ue* en aquello ay exemplo para quien teme.

[1] MS: dešenbolo.
[2] MS: akaaska.
[3] MS: šenbelante.

ءَأَنتُمْ أَشَدُّ خَلْقًا أَمِ ٱلسَّمَآءُ بَنَىٰهَا

27

What, are you stronger in constitution or the heaven He built?

BN 5078: E aši ¿šoš bošotroš de maš fwerte ẖaleqamyento, o el syelo ke lo[1] frawó šinše pilareš?

P 425: I ¿šoyš bošotroš de maš fwerte ẖaleqamyento, o el syelo ke lo fragó šinše pilareš?

J 39: E aši ¿šoyš bošotroš maš fwerteš, o el syelo ke lo fragó šin pilareš?

J 25: Pweš e aši ¿šoyš bošotroš de maš fwerte ẖaleqamyento, o el syelo ke lo fragwó?

BN 4938: Pweš ¿šoeš bošotroš de maš fwerte ẖaleqamyento, o el syelo ke lo fragwé šineš de pilareš?

T 235: Dixo Allah, "¿Sois vosotros de mas fuerte ћalecamiento, o el çielo y su fraguaçion?"

[1] MS: la.

رَفَعَ سَمْكَهَا فَسَوَّىٰهَا

28

He lifted up its vault, and levelled it,

BN 5078: I lebantó šu altura andadura de sinsyentoš annoš;

P 425: I lebantó šu alteza andadura de[1] šeysyentoš annoš;

J 39: I alsó šu altura andadura de šeyššyentoš annoš;

J 25: I alsó šu šoštenimyento šinše pilareš i šu altura i lo konpušo;

BN 4938: I lebanta šu altaryo sinsyentoš annoš d-andadura;

T 235: *Que* alçó su sostenimiento y alteça y los emparejó;

[1] MS: da.

وَأَغْطَشَ لَيْلَهَا وَأَخْرَجَ ضُحَاهَا

29

and darkened its night, and brought forth its forenoon;

BN 5078: y-eškuresyo šu nwey, i šakó la klaredat del šol;

P 425: y-eškeresyo šu nweyte, i šakó la klaredat del šol;

J 39: y-eškuresyo šu noče, i šaka la klaredad del šol;

J 25: y-eškurasyo šu noče, i šakó la klaredad del šol;

BN 4938: i eškareskó la noče, i šakó la klaredat del šol;

T 235: y escureçio su noche, y sacó su sol y rresplandor;

وَالْأَرْضَ بَعْدَ ذَٰلِكَ دَحَاهَا

30

and the earth —after that He spread it out,

BN 5078: y-ešpandyo apreš de akello la tyerra šobr-el agwa [1].

P 425: y-ešpandyo apreš de akello la tyerra šobre ell [a]gwa [2].

J 39: y-ešpandyo depweš de akello la tyerra šobre ell agwa [3].

J 25: i la tyerra depweš de akello eštendyola.

BN 4938: a la tyerra apre[š] [4] de akello ešpandola šobre ell agwa.

T 235: y la tierra despues de aquello tendiola.

---

1 MS: aguwa.
2 MS: ell guwa.
3 MS: awaguwa.
4 End of line blurred in MS.

أخرج منها ماءها ومرعيها

31

therefrom brought forth its waters and its pastures,

BN 5078: Šaka de la tyerra šu awa i šuš yerbaš,

P 425: Šakó de la tyerra šu awa i šuš yerbaš,

J 39: Šaka d-ella —kyere dezir de la tyerra— šu agwa [1] i šuš yerbaš,

J 25: I šakó d-ella šu agwa [1] i šuš yerbaš,

BN 4938: I šakó Allah de la tyerra šu agwa i šuš yerbaš,

T 235: Y sacó della su agua y sus pastos,

[1] MS: aguwa.

والجبال أرسيها

32

and the mountains He set firm,

BN 5078: i loš monteš mišološ rrefirmamyento d-ella,

P 425: i loš monteš pušološ rrefirmamyento d-ella,

J 39: i loš monteš pušološ rrefirmamyento d-ella,

J 25: i loš monteš pušološ rrefirmamyento d-ella,

BN 4938: en loš monteš pušološ rrefirmamyento d-ella,

T 235: y los montes asentolos,

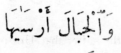

مَتَاعًا لَكُمْ وَلِأَنْعَامِكُمْ

33

an enjoyment for you and your flocks.

BN 5078: porke šia ešpleyt a elloš, a bošotroš, i a bweštroš ganadoš dakía la mwerte.

P 425: porke šea ešpleyte a bošotroš y-a bweštroš ganadoš dakía la mwerte.

J 39: para dešpleyte a bošotroš y-a bweštroš ganadoš hata la mwerte.

J 25: para ke šea ešpleyte a bošotroš y-a bweštroš ganadoš.

BN 4938: ešpleyte para bošotroš i a bweštroš ganadoš fašta la mwerte.

T 235: espleyte a vosotros y a v*uest*ros animales.

فَإِذَا جَاءَتِ الطَّامَّةُ الْكُبْرَى

34

Then, when the Great Catastrophe comes

BN 5078: I kwando beran la fortuna mayor, ke šera el šoflo del kwerno la sagera begada, kwando trayran de loš del alğanna al alğanna i loš del fwego al fwego;

P 425: I kwando benrra la fortuna mayor, ke šera el šoflo del kwerno la sagera begad[a] [1], kwando traeran loš del alğanna al alğanna i loš del fwego al fwego;

J 39: Pweš kwando bendra la fortuna mayor, ke šera el šoflo del kwerno sagero, kwando trayran loš de alğannah al alğannah i loš del fwego al fwego;

J 25: Pweš kwando berna la fortuna mayor, ke šera el šoflo del kwerno;

BN 4938: I kwando beran la fwerte fortuna mayor, šera el šoflo de la tronpa sagero, kwando trayran loš de la glorya alğanna i loš del fwego el fwego;

T 235: Pues quando vendra la fortuna mayor,

1 MS blurred.

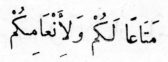

يَوْمَ يَتَذَكَّرُ ٱلْإِنسَانُ مَا سَعَىٰ

35

upon the day when man shall remember what he has striven,

BN 5078: el dia ke še rrekordará la prešona ke-l tomarán konto de šuš obraš de lo ke abrá obrado;

P 425: el dia ke tomarán kwento de šuš obraš i de lo ke abrán obrado;

J 39: el dia ke še rrekordará la peršona de lo ke abrá obrado;

J 25: el dia ke še rrekordará la peršona de lo ke abrá obrado;

BN 4938: i še rrekordará la prešona de lo ke a obrado;

T 235: aquel dia se acordará la persona de lo q*ue* abrá obrado;

بُرِّزَتِ ٱلْجَحِيمُ لِمَن يَرَىٰ

36

and Hell is advanced for whoever sees,

BN 5078: y-eškubriršе a ǧahannam kon la pena a kyen bera de loš maloš;

P 425: y-eškrubirše[1] a ǧahannam kon la pena a kyen bera de loš maloš;

J 39: i deškubrirše a ǧahannam kon la pena a kyen bera de loš maloš;

J 25: y-eškubrirše a ǧahannam a kyen bera de loš maloš;

BN 4938: i eškubriršа ǧahannam kon la pena para kyen la bera de loš maloš;

T 235: y escubrirse a chehannam para quien vera de los malos;

---

1 MS: eškurubirše.

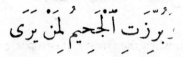

فَأَمَّا مَن طَغَىٰ

37

then as for him who was insolent

BN 5078: a kwanto kyen šera deškonesyent

P 425: a kwanto kyen šera deškonosyent

J 39: a kwanto kyen šera deškonosido

J 25: a kwanto kyen šera deškonosido

BN 4938: a kwanto kyen deškreyerá

T 235: a quanto quien no creera

وَءَاثَرَ ٱلْحَيَوٰةَ ٱلدُّنْيَا

38

and preferred the present life,

BN 5078: i bantallará la bida de akešte mundo i no kreyerá kon la otro,

P 425: i abantallará la bida d-ešte mundo i no kyeren kon el otro mundo,

J 39: i abantallará la bida d-ešte mundo i no kreera kon el otro,

J 25: y-abantallará la bida de akešte mundo,

BN 4938: i abantağará la bida de akešte mundo i no kreyerá kon ell otro mundo,

T 235: y abentajará la vida deste mundo sobre el otro,

فَإِنَّ ٱلْجَحِيمَ هِىَ ٱلْمَأْوَىٰ

39

surely Hell shall be the refuge.

BN 5078: pweš el fwego šera[1] šu kaša i šošyego.

P 425: pweš el fwego šera šu kaša i šošyego.

J 39: pwe[š] el fwego eš [šu] šošyego.

J 25: pweš el fwego šera šu šošyego.

BN 4938: pweš el fwego šera šu kaša[2].

T 235: pues chehannam sera su asitiada.

---

1 MS: šera šera.
2 MS: šera šk šu kaša.

وَأَمَّا مَنْ خَافَ مَقَامَ رَبِّهِ وَنَهَى ٱلنَّفْسَ عَنِ ٱلْهَوَىٰ

40

But as for him who feared the Station of his Lord and forbade the soul its caprice,

BN 5078: I kyen abrá myedo al porparamyento de šu šennor i debedará šu prešona de šegir šu boluntat,

P 425: I kyen a myedo al prometimyento de šu šennor i debedará a šu prešona de šegir šu boluntad,

J 39: A kwanto kyen abrá myedo al porparamyento de šu šennor i debedará šu peršona de šegir šu boluntad,

J 25: A kwanto kyen abrá myedo al porparamyento delante de šu šennor i debeda šu peršona de šegir šu boluntad,

BN 4938: A kwanto kyen abrá myedo el paramyento de Allah šu šennor bedará šu prešona de šegir šu boluntad,

T 235: A quanto quien creera y temera la parada delante de su señor i detendra su persona de los apetitos,

$$ \text{فَاِنَّ ٱلْجَنَّةَ هِىَ ٱلْمَأْوَى} $$

41

surely Paradise shall be the refuge.

BN 5078:

P 425:   pweš el alğanna šera šu šošyego.

J 39:   pweš el alğannah eš [šu] šošyego.

J 25:   pweš el alğanna eš šu šošyego [1].

BN 4938: pweš la glorya šera šu ašentamyento.

T 235:   pues el alchanna sera su asitiada.

---

[1] MS: ššošiyego.

$$ \text{يَسْئَلُونَكَ عَنِ ٱلسَّاعَةِ أَيَّانَ مُرْسِيهَا} $$

42

They will question thee concerning the Hour, when it shall berth.

BN 5078:

P 425:   Aun te demandarán por el dia del ğwisyo kwando a de plegar i a de
            šer šu rrefirmamyento.

J 39:   Aun te demandarán, yā Muḥammad, por el dia del ğudisyo kwando
            šera šu rrefirmamyento.

J 25:   Demandarte an, yā Muḥammad, por el dia del ğudisyo kwando a de
            šer šu rrefirmamyento.

BN 4938: I aun te demandoron por el dia del ğudisyo ke kwando a de plegar o
            de šeyer šu rrefirmamyento —ešto š-e[nt]yende [1] ke demandaban
            mučo al allannabī, ʿalayhi is-salāmu, ke kwando abia de šer el dia del
            ğudisyo.

T 235:   Dixo, "Demandarte an, ye Muhamed, por el dia del judiçio en que
            tiempo sera su afirmamiento.

---

[1] Dots on *nūn* and *tā'* omitted in MS.

فِيمَ أَنْتَ مِنْ ذِكْرَاهَا

43 What art thou about, to mention it?

BN 5078:

P 425: Pweš ¿en ke-štaš tu? ke kwando abia de šer el đia del ğwisyo.

J 39: Pweš ¿en ke-štaš tu de šu nonbramyento? —kišo dezir el annabī, porke demandaba mučo ke kwando abia de šer el dia del ğudisyo.

J 25: Y-¿en ke eštaš tu de šu nonbramyento?

BN 4938: Dišo Allah, "Yā Muḥammad, ¿en ke eštaš tu šu lonbramyento?

T 235: Y ¿en *que* estas tu, ye Muhamed, de su nombramiento?

إِلَىٰ رَبِّكَ مُنْتَهَاهَا

44 Unto thy Lord is the final end of it.

BN 5078:

P 425: I no le fwe feyto a šaber kon ello. Ada Allah eš el šaber de la fin del ğwisyo.

J 39: [I?][1] le fwe hečo a šaber kon el ke ada Allah eš el šaber de la fin del ğudisyo.

J 25: Dileš, "A tu šennor eš el plegar al kabo d-ello".

BN 4938: Ada Allah eš el fin del ğudisyo kwando a de šeyer.

T 235: *Que* a tu señor, ye Muhamed, es el saber de la fin del judiçio.

---

1 MS very blurred.

إنما أنت منذر من يخشيها

45

Thou art only the warner of him who fears it.

BN 5078:

P 425: I tu no fweš[te] enbyado šino pedrikador ke abyešen myedo de la pena d-Allah en akel dia; i no lo rresibe de tu šino kyen lo temera.

J 39: Ke tu [no?] [1] fwešte enbyado šino por preika[dor] [2] porke ayan myedo a la pena de Allah en akel dia i no lo rresibe [de?] [1] tu šino [kyen lo?] [1] temera.

J 25: Ke no ereš tu šino pedrikador a kyen teme ada Allah parad akel dia.

BN 4938: Ke tu, yā Muḥammad, no fušte enbyado šino pedrikador i monešteyador a kyen le a d-aber myedo.

T 235: Empero tu eres monestador a quien tema al dia del judiçio.

---

1 MS very blurred throughout.
2 MS: pereika ... (rest blurred).

كأنهم يوم يرونها لم يلبثوا إلا عشية أو ضحيها

46

It shall be as if, on the day they see it, they have but tarried for an evening, or its forenoon.

BN 5078:

P 425: Komo akelloš el dia del ǧwisyo ke lo beran no leš paresen ke fweron en el mundo šino komo una ora o rrato de la tarde o de la mannana.

J 39: Ke elloš el dia ke lo beran no leš pareseran ke fweron en el mundo šino komo un rrato de la tarde [o] de la mannana.

J 25: I šera komo ke elloš el dia ke lo beran no leš paresera ke fweron en el mundo šino komo un rrato de la tarde o de la mannana.

BN 4938: Ke elloš el dia ke lo beran no še leš paresera ke fweron en el mundo šino komo una tarde o una mannanada".

T 235: Pareçerseles a el dia q*ue* la veran q*ue* no estubieron en el mundo sino como vna ora de la tarde o de la mañana".

V. Glossary.

The Glossary is exhaustive, and lists every occurrence of each word in the texts. The only exceptions are a few very common forms such as definite articles and the conjunction *i* (*y*), for which only the first five locations are given. Adjectives are listed in the masculine singular form, though if they occur in the text only in a different person or number, it is so stated. The gender of nouns is recorded only if it can be unequivocally established from these particular texts. Separate entries have been made for the infinitives of verbs and, if they occur, for past participles, present participles, and gerunds.

Alphabetization obeys English, rather than Spanish, order. Ǧ follows G; Ḥ and Ḫ, both transliterations of Arabic consonants, follow H. Orthographic variants of a single item are grouped together in order of their statistical frequency in these texts, and are also cross-referenced. Many such variants come from T 235, the only MS in Latin script, and are easily recognizable by their "modern" spelling, e. g. AQUELLO as against AKẸḶLO. In such obvious cases, the variant is not singled out in the body of the entry: that is, under AKẸḶLO/AQUẸḶLO (q. v.), any citation from T 235 may be assumed to have the latter spelling.

Each entry is organized as follows: (a) word or phrase from the text; (b) part of speech; (c) meaning(s), in single quotes; (d) cross-reference to synonyms, if any; (e) location(s) in the text, consisting of Qur'ān verse (an italic Arabic numeral) followed by manuscript number(s), e. g. *15*: 4938, *43*: 39. Where a form is found in all six MSS, the verse number is succeeded by the word "all". Where applicable, an entry may further include: (f) other Aljamiado or Aragonese texts displaying the word at issue (for meanings of abbreviations, see the Bibliography); (g) bibliographic references; and (h) miscellaneous comments.

Arabic and Romance words have been included in the same listing; Arabic phrases or formulas appear under their first word.

A/Ada: prep.: 'to'. W. personal d. o.: *19*: 5078, 39, 25, 235, *26*: 25; w. non-personal d. o: *21*: 5078, 39, *30*: 4938, *40*: 425, *45*: 25, 235; w. ind. o.: *15*: 4938, *17*: 5078, 425, 39, 25, *26*: 5078, 425, 39, 4938, *36*: 5078, 425, 39, 25, *42*: 4938. 'Direction toward': *17, 19*: all, *22*: 5078, 425, *45*: 25, 4938; 'end-point of movement': *16*: 235, *34*: 5078, 425, 39, *44*: 25; possession or attribution (e. g., *ada Allah eš* 'to God belongs'): *18*: 4938, 235, *44*: 425, 39, 25, 4938, 235; purpose: *14*: 4938, *18*: 25; 'for (the benefit of)': *26*: 5078, 425, *33*: all. Phrases: *tornadoš a ḫaleqar* (*rrebibkar*) 'created (resurrected) again': *10*: 25, 4938; *emoš a šeyer* 'we will be': *10*: 5078; *dar a ber* 'to show': *20*: 39, 25, 235; *hečo* (*feyto*) *a šaber* 'made known': *44*: 425, 39; *aber myedo a* 'to fear': *40*: 5078, 425, 39, 25, *45*: 39; *a la fe* 'indeed': *13*: 235; *a kwanto* 'as for': *37*: all, *40*: 39, 25, 4938, 235. *Ad* is Aragonese: Alvar, *Dial.*, 250. *Batallas* 2v 10 *ada*; *Alj. T.* J 3 id.

[Abansarše]: v. refl.: 'to put o. s. forward' [cf. Adebantarše, Adelantarše]. *Še abansaron 4*: 4938.

[Abantallar/Abantağar/Abentajar]: v. trans.: 'to prefer, favor' [cf. Bantallar]. *Abantallará 38*: 425, 39, 25, *abantağará 38*: 4938, *abentajará 38*: 235. *Alj. T.* J 3 *abantağar, ibantalla* (n.); *Batallas, avantaja.*

Aber/[Haber]: v. 'to have'. Pres. ind.: *a 40*: 425; fut.: *abrá 26*: 5078, 39, 4938, *40*: 5078, 39, 25, 4938; pres. subj.: *ayaš 19*: 4938; imperf. subj.: *abyešen*: *45*: 425; imper.: *abe 19*: 425, *aw 19*: 5078. (Cf. *abe* 'hay', *P. Yúçuf* A 28 d.) Aux. w. p. ptc.: *a 15*: 4938, *17*: 5078, 39, 25, 4938, *18*: 5078, 425, 39, 25, *35*: 4938, *abrá 35*: 5078, 39, 25, 235, *abrán 35*: 425. Impersonal ('there is, are', etc.): *ay 26*: 425, 39, 25, 4938, 235, *abrá 7*: 5078, 425, 39, *8*: all. *A. de* & inf. (obligation or necessity): *aber 45*: 4938, *a 42*: 425, 25, 4938, *44, 45*: 4938, *abemoš 10*: 4938, *habemos 10*: 235, *emos 10*: 425, 39, 25, *abia 42*: 4938, *43*: 425, 39, *ayan 45*: 39. *A. a* & inf. (id.): *emoš 10*: 5078.

[Acordarse]: v. refl.: 'to remember' [cf. Rrekordarše]. *Se acordará* (*de*) *35*: 235.

Ada: [v. A].

Ad(d)īn: n.: 'religion' (Ar. *ad-dīn*). *Addin 19*: 5078, *addīn 19*: 425, 39, 25, *adin 19*: 235. *Alj. T.* J 3; *Batallas* 9v 2; *R. Ališ.* 37v.

[Adebantarše]: v. refl.: 'to put o. s. forward' [cf. Abansarše, Adelantarše, Debantarše]. *Še adebantor*[*o*]*n 4*: 5078. *R. Ališ.* 67v *adebantar.*

Adelanta-myento/-miento: n. m.: 'going forward'. *4*: 25, 235.

Adelantante: pres. ptc. used as n.: 'one who goes forward". *Adelantantes 4*: 235.

[Adelantarše]: v. refl.: 'to put o. s. forward' [cf. Abansarše, Adebantarše, Debantarše]. *Še adelantaron 4*: 25, 235.

Afirmamiento: n. m.: 'establishment' [cf. Rrefirmamyento]. *42*: 235.

[Afogar/Ahogar]: v.: 'to drown'. *Afogó 25*: 5078, 425, 25, 4938, *ahogó 25*: 39.

Afollamyento: n. m.: 'haste'. *22*: 5078, 39, 4938; *la follamyenta 22*: 425 is clearly a misreading of *afollamyento*. For this meaning see C. López-Morillas, *Actas*, 366-367; cf. *afollar* 'to destroy' *Alj. T.* J 3, *R. Ališ.* 15; *P. Yúçuf* A 52c.

Agwa/Awa/Agua: n.: 'water'. *Agwa 30*: 5078, 425, 39, 4938, *31*: 39, 25, 4938; *awa 31*: 5078, 425; *agua 31*: 235.

Ahogar: [v. Afogar].

[Akaeser]: v.: 'to befall'. *Akaesyo 26*: 5078, 425, 39, 4938, *akaeska 26*: 5078, 425, 39, 4938.

Akel/Aquel: demonstr. m.: 'that'. Pron.: *12*: 4938, *20*: 5078, 425, 39. Adj.: *8*: all, *12*: 5078, 425, 39, *16*: 4938, *35*: 235, *45*: 425, 39, 25.

Akella/Aquella: demonstr. f.: 'that'. Pron.: *12*: 35, 235. Adj.: *12*: 4938.

Akello/Aquello: demonstr. pron. neut.: 'that'. *12*: 425, *24*: 4938, *26, 30*: 425, 39, 25, 4938, 235.

Akelloš: demonstr. pron. m. pl.: 'those'. *9*: 5078, 425, 4938, *46*: 425.

Akešte: demonstr. m.: 'this' [cf. Ešte]. Pron.: *25*: 5078, 425, 25. Adj.: *38*: 5078, 25, 4938. *Batallas* 57v 4.

Akešta: demonstr. pron. f.: 'this'. *25*: 39.

ᶜALAYHI IS-SALĀMU: Ar. formula: 'peace be upon him' (after the name of the Prophet). *42*: 4938.
ALÇAR: [v. ALSAR].
ALĞANNA(H)/ALCHANNA: n.: 'Paradise' (Ar. *al-janna*) [cf. GLORYA]. *34*: 5078, 425, 39, 4938, *41*: 425, 39, 25, 235. *Alj. T.* J 3; *L. Yūsuf* 113; *R. Ališ.* 21.
[ALINPYARŠE]: v. refl.: 'to cleanse o. s.'. *Te alinpyeš 18*: 25. *L. Yūsuf* 188; *Alj. T.* J 3 *alinpi(y)ar*.
ALLAH n. pr. m.: 'God.' *1, 4, 5*: 5078, 425, 25, 4938, 235, *8*: 4938, *13*: 5078, 425, 39, 25, 4938, *15*: 25, 4938, *17, 18, 21*: 5078, 425, 39, 25, 4938, *19*: 5078, 425, 39, 25, *24*: 4938, *25*: all, *26*: 25, *27*: 235, *31, 40, 43*: 4938, *44*: 425, 39, 4938, *45*: 425, 39, 25.
ALLANNABĪ: [v. ANNABĪ].
ALMALAK(E)/ALMALAQUE: n. m.: 'angel' (Ar. *al-malak*). *Almalakeš 2, 4*: 5078, 425, 25, 4938, 235, *5*: 5078, 425, 25, 235. *P. Yúçuf* B 89, *Alj. T.* J 3. The exact form of the singular here remains uncertain. The *Alj. T.* show both *almalak* (BN 5053) and *almalake* (J 3: 87v 6), *almalaqe* (J 3: 206v 6).
[ALSAR]: v.: 'to raise' [cf. LEBANTAR]. *Alsó 27*: 25, *28*: 39, 235.
ALTARYO: n. m.: 'height' [cf. ALT-EÇA, -EZA, ALTURA]. *28*: 4938.
ALT-EÇA/-EZA: n.: 'height' [cf. ALTARYO, ALTURA]. *28*: 425, 235.
ALTO: adj.: 'high'. *24*: 4938.
ALTURA: n.: 'height' [cf. ALTARYO, ALT-EÇA, -EZA]. *28*: 5078, 39, 25.
AMEDRESIDO: adj.: 'frightened' [cf. TEMEROŠO]. *Amedresidoš 9*: 4938. *Alj. T.* J 3 *amedresedor.* The form clearly belongs with the other adjectival formations in *-ido* (often related to *-ecer* verbs) whose meaning contains some idea of privation (weakness, fear, hunger, etc.): cf. *desmedrido* 'downhearted', *esmedrido* 'frightened', both from *Alex.* O. See Y. Malkiel, *Lg.*, XXII (1946), 284-316, esp. 302-309.
ANDADURA: n.: 'time required to walk a given distance'. *28*: 5078, 425, 39, 4938. *R. Ališ.* 4; *Alj. T.* J 3; *Batallas,* 20v 4. On the suffix *-ura see* Y. Malkiel, *Lg.*, XXI (1945), 165 nn. 233 & 234.
ANDAMIENTO: n.: 'going'. *3*: 235.
ANDANTE: pres. ptc. used as n.: 'goer'. *Andantes 3*: 235.
[ANDAR]: v.: 'to go'. *Andan 3*: 5078, 425, 25, 4938, 235.
ANIMAL: n. m.: 'animal'. *Animales 33*: 235.
ANNABĪ: n. m.: 'the Prophet' (Ar. *an-nabī*) [cf. MUḤAMMAD]. *15*: 4938, *43*: 39. *Allannabī 42*: 4938. *Alj. T.* J 3; *Batallas* 1r 3; *R. Ališ.* 1.
ANNO: n. m.: 'year'. *Annoš 7, 28*: 5078, 425, 39, 4938.
ANTEŠ: adv. (preceded by *de*): 'before'. *20*: 4938.
APETITO: n. m.: 'appetite'. *Apetitos 40*: 235.
APREŠ: adv.: 'afterward'; prep. (followed by *de*) 'after' [cf. DEPWEŠ, LWEGO, TRAS]. *7*: 5078, 425, 25, 4938, *30*: 5078, 425, 4938. *R. Ališ.* 28; *Alj. T.* J 64; *L. Regum* 3.3; Umphrey.
AQUEL: [v. AKEL].
AQUELLA: [v. AKELLA].
AQUELLO: [v. AKELLO].
ARRANKA-MYENTO/-MIENTO: n.: 'pulling, plucking out'. *2*: 25, 235.
ARRANCANTE: pres. ptc. used as n.: 'one who pulls or plucks out". *Arrancantes 2*: 235.
[ARRANKAR]: v.: 'to pull, pluck out' [cf. RRANKAR]. *Arrankan 2*: 5078, 25, 4938, 235.
ARRUḤ/ARRŪH/ARROH: n. m.: 'soul' (Ar. *ar-rūḥ*). *Arruḥeš 2*: 5078, 425, 4938, *arrūheš 2*: 25, *arrohes 2*: 235. *Alj. T.* J 3; *Batallas* 3r 6; *L. Yūsuf* 176.
AŠENTAMYENTO: n.: '(resting-) place' [cf. ASITIADA, ŠOŠYEGO]. *41*: 4938.
[ASENTAR]: v.: 'to make firm'. *Asentó 32*: 235.
AŠI: adv.: 'thus, so'. *16*: 5078, 425, 39, 4938, *18*: 25, *27*: 5078, 25, 39.
ASITIADA: n.: '(resting-) place' [cf. AŠENTAMYENTO, ŠOŠYEGO]. *39, 41*: 235. *Batallas* T 18. Cf. Borao, *sitiada* 'junta de gobierno'. Ultimately from OProv. *assetiar* 'to place, establish'; Cat.-Val. *sitiada* 'session' shows that *(a)sitiar* once had the meaning 'to seat'. *DCELC,* s. v. *sitio.*
AUN: adv.: 'yet'. *10*: 5078, 425, 39, 25, 4938, *42*: 425, 39, 4938.
AW: [v. ABER].
AWA: [v. AGWA].
BAL: n. m.: 'valley'. *16*: all. *L. Yūsuf* 2.
[BANTALLAR]: v. trans.: 'to prefer, favor' [cf. ABANTALLAR, ABANTAĞAR]. *Bantallará 38*: 5078. *Alj. T.* J 3 *bantağa, R. Ališ.* 75 id.
[BAŠAR]: v.: 'to descend'. *Bašan 5*: 5078, 425, 25, 4938.

BAŠILLO/BAŠYELLO/VAXILLO: n. m.: 'ship'. *Baš-illoš 3*: 425, 25, *-yelloš 3*: 5078, 4938, *vaxillos 3*: 235. *L. Yūsuf* 17 *bašillo* 'vessel, container'; *Alj. T.* J 13 *baši(y)ello,* J 3 *bašillo* 'id.'.
BAŠYELLO: [v. BAŠILLO].
[BEDAR]: v.: 'to forbid' [cf. DEBEDAR]. *Bedará 40*: 4938.
BEGADA: n. f.: 'time (i. e., occasion)' [cf. BEŠ]. *34*: 5078, 425. *P. Yūçuf* A55c; *L. Yūsuf* 16; *Alj. T.* J 3; *F. Teruel* 14 *uegada.*
[BENIR/VENIR]: v.: 'to come'. *Benrra 34*: 425, *berna 34*: 25, *bendra 34*: 39, *vendra 34*: 235; *bino 15*: 5078, 425, 39, 25, *vino 15*: 235. *Batallas* 78r 3 *verná.*
BEOŠ/VEOS: interj.: 'behold!' *14*: 39, 25, *veos 14*: 235. *R. Ališ.* 30v; *L. Yūsuf 20*; *Alj. T.* J 3; *Batallas* 3v 15 *veos.*
BER/VER: v.: 'to see'. *Ber 20*: 39, 25, *ver 20*: 235; *bera 36*: 5078, 425, 39, 25, 4938, *vera 36*: 235, *beran 34*: 5078, 4938, *46*: 425, 39, 25, 4938, *veran 46*: 235; *beamoš 10*: 425, 39, 25, *beyamoš*: 5078, 4938.
BERDADERAMENT(E): adv.: 'truly'. *-Nt 13*: 5078, 4938, *-nte 13*: 425.
BERNA: [v. BENIR].
BEŠ: n. f.: 'time (i. e., occasion)' [cf. BEGADA]. *20*: 4938.
BEŠ: [v. IR].
BIDA/VIDA: n. f.: 'life'. *25*: 39, 235, *38*: all.
BIŠTA/VISTA: n. f.: 'sight; look'. *20*: 4938; *bištaš* 9: 39, 25, 235.
BLANKO: adj.: 'white'. *Blanka 20*: 5078, 425, 39.
[BOLBER(ŠE)/VOLBER]: v. (refl.): 'to turn (around)' [cf. RRETORNARŠE, TORNAR(SE)]. *Bolbyoše 22*: 39, 25, *volbio 22*: 235.
BOLUNTA-D/-T: n.: 'will'. *-D 40*: 425, 39, 25, 235, *-t 40*: 5078.
BOŠOTROŠ/VOSOTROS: str. pers. pron.: 'you' (pl.). *27, 33*: all.
BOZINA/VOZINA: n. f.: 'horn, trumpet' [cf. KWERNO, TRONPA]. *6*: 5078, 425, 39, 25, 4938, *13*: all.
BWEŠTRO/VUESTRO: poss. adj.: 'your' (pl.). *24*: all, *bweštroš 33*: all.
CARA: [v. KARA].
CHEHANNAM: [v. ĞAHANNAM].
ÇIELO: [v. SYELO].
COMO: interrog. adv.: 'how?' [cf. KOMO 'as']. *10*: 235.
COMPREHENDER: [v. KONPRENDER].
CON: [v. KON].
CORAZON: [v. KORASON].
CREER: [v. KREER].
CREYENTE: [v. KREYENTE].
CUESTA: n. f.: (in pl.) 'back (of person's body)'. *Cuestas 22*: 235. *P. Yúçuf* B 84a; *Alj. T.* J 59; *F. Arag.* 2, 1 *itar ... tras cuestas* 'echarse a las espaldas, olvidar'.
D-: [v. DE].
DAKÍA: prep. 'until' [cf. HATA, FAŠTA]. *33*: 5078, 425. *R. Ališ.*, frequent; *P. Yúçuf* A 46c *dakiʸ-a ke*; *Alj. T.* BN 4944. See A. Castro, *RFE*, III (1915), 182; and *DCELC*, s. v. *aquí.*
DAR: v.: 'to give'. *Dar 14*: 4938, *dio a ber* 'he showed' *20*: 39, 25, 235.
DE/D-: prep.: 'of' (possession, attribution): *2*: 5078, 425, 25, 235, *5*: 4938, *6*: 4938, 235, *9*: 5078, 425, 4938, *12*: 4938, *14*: 5078, 425, 39, 25, 235, *18*: 25, 39, *19*: 5078, 425, 39, 25, 235, *20*: 4938, *21*: 5078, 425, 4938, *25*: all, *29*: 5078, 425, 39, 25, 4938, *34*: 5078, 425, 39, 4938, *35*: 5078, 425, *38*: all, *40*: 5078, 425, 39, 4938, *42*: 425, 39, 25, 4938, 235, *43*: 39, *44*: 425, 39, 25, 4938, 235, *45*: 425, 39, 235, *46*: 425, 39, 25, 235. 'About, concerning': *5*: 4938, *15*: all, *43*: 39, 25, 235, *44*: 425, 39, 235. 'From' (point of origin): *1*: all, *20*: 5078, 39, 425, *22*: 5078, 425, 39, 25, 4938, *31*: all, *45*: 425. 'Toward, due to': *4*: all, *19*: 4938. 'By reason of': *8*: 4938. Classification: *12*: 235, *16*: all, *20*: 5078, 425, 39, 25. 'Made of, consisting of': *20*: 4938, *27*: 5078, 425, 25, 4938, 235, *28*: 5078, 425, 39, 4938. 'Among': *20*: 5078, 39, 4938. 'For the benefit of': *32*: 5078, 425, 39, 25, 4938. After other prepositions (*apreš, delante, de(š)pweš,* etc.): *7*: 5078, 425, 39, 25, 235, *11*: 4938, *30*: all, *40*: 25, 235. *De anteš* (adv.) 'before, earlier': *20*: 4938. *Semeğante, senblante de* 'the likes of': *26*: 5078, 39, 4938. *Aber de* & inf. 'to have to': *10*: 425, 39, 25, 4938, 235, *42*: 425, 25, 4938, *44, 45*: 4938; *aber myedo de 19, 45*: 425. *Rrek-, ac-ordarše de* 'to recall': *35*: 39, 25, 4938, 235. *De-bedar, -tener de* 'to withhold from': *40*: all. Partitive: *34*: 5078, *36*: all.
[DEBANTARŠE]: v. refl.: 'to put o. s. forward' [cf. ABANSARŠE, ADEBANTARSE, ADELANTARŠE]. *Še debantaron 4*: 425. *Alj. T.* J 3 *debantar, -še.*
[DEBEDAR]: v.: 'to forbid' [cf. BEDAR]. *Debeda 40*: 25; *debedará 40*: 5078, 425, 39. *Alj. T.* J 3; *Batallas* 87v 12; *R. Ališ.* 37v.

DELANTE: prep.: (followed by *de*) 'in front of'. *40*: 25, 235.
[DEMANDAR]: v.: 'to ask, demand'. *Demandaba 43*: 39, *demandaban 42*: 4938; *demandarán 42*: 425, 39, *demandarte an 42*: 25, 235; *demandoron 42*: 4938.
[DEMOŠTRAR]: v.: 'to show'. *Demweštra 20*: 425; *demoštro 20*: 5078, 4938.
DEPWEŠ/DESPUES: adv.: 'afterward'; prep. (followed by *de* or *ke*): 'after' [cf. APRES, LWEGO]. *7*: 39, *10*: 425, 39, *11*: 5078, 39, 25, 4938, *20*: 4938, *22*: 25, 235, *30*: 39, 25, 235. *Depweš* in *L. Yūsuf* 6; *Alj. T.* J 3; *F. Teruel* (B)2; *Vidal* I, 18; Alvar, *T. dial.* See R. J. Cuervo, *DCR,* II, 1164-1165.
[DEŠANPARAR]: v.: 'to abandon'. *Dešanparó 25*: 39.
[DESCONOÇER]: v.: 'to disbelieve' [cf. DEŠKREYER]. *Desconoçe 17*: 235.
DEŠKONOSIDO: n. or adj.: 'unbelieving' [cf. DEŠKONOSYENT, DEŠKREIDO]. *37*: 39, 25.
DEŠKONOSYENT: pres. ptc.: 'unbelieving' [cf. DEŠKONOSIDO, DEŠKREIDO]. *37*: 425; *deškonesyent 37*: 5078. For the *-esyent* variant cf. *R. Ališ.* 66 *koneser.*
DEŠKRE(Y)IDO: p. ptc.: 'disbelieved': *17*: 5078, 39, 25, 39; adj.: 'unbelieving' [cf. DEŠKONOSYENT, DEŠKONOSIDO]: *17*: 425.
DEŠKREYENTE/DESCREYENTE: pres. ptc. used as n.: 'unbeliever'. *Deškreyenteš 10*: all, *12*: 5078, 425, 39, 4938.
[DEŠKREYER]: v.: 'to disbelieve' [cf. DESCONOÇER]. *Deškreyerá 37*: 4938. *Batallas* 75v 13.
DEŠKUBRIRŠE: v. refl.: 'to revealed' [cf. EŠKUBRIRSE]. *Deškubriršе a 36*: 39.
DEŠMENTIR: v.: 'to deny; to declare something to be a lie' [cf. EŠMENTIR]. *Dešmentir 12*: 5078, 39, *dešmintyo 21*: 25, 235. *Alj. T.* J 3 *dešmentimi(y)ento*; *F. Teruel* 110.
[DEŠOBEDESER]: v.: 'to disobey'. *Dešobedesyo 21*: all.
DEŠPLEYTE: n.: 'provision' [cf. EŠPLEYT(E)]. *33*: 39. *Alj. T.* J 3 *dešp(e)lleite.*
DESPUES: [v. DEPWEŠ].
DEŠ(Š)ENPLO: n. m.: 'example' [cf. EXEMPLO, INŠ(Y)ENPLO]. *26*: 5078, 39. 25. *Alj. T.* J 3.
[DETENER]: v.: 'to withhold'. *Detendrá 40*: 235.
DETERMINASYON: n. f.: 'definition'. *5*: 4938.
DEZIR: v.: 'to say, tell'. Inf.: *31, 43*: 39; pres. ind.: *dize 13*: 5078, 39, 25, 4938, *15*: 25, *diz' 13*: 425, *dizen 10*: 5078, 425, 39, 25, 4938, *12*: 5078, 425, 39, 25, 235; imperf.: *deçian 10*: 235; pret.: *dišo 15, 17*: 4938, *17*: 5078, 425, 25, *24*: 5078, 425, 25, 4938, *43*: 4938, *diššo 17, 24*: 39, *dixo 13, 15, 17, 24, 27, 42*: 235, *dixeron 12*: 235; imper.: *di 18*: all, *44*: 25.
DIA: n. m.: 'day'. *6, 8*: all, *35*: 5078, 425, 39, 25, 235, *42, 46*: 425, 39, 25, 4938, 235, *43*: 425, 39, *45*: 425, 39, 25, 235.
E: conj.: 'and' [cf. I]. *1, 13, 14*: 5078, *18*: 25, *20*: 4938, *27*: 5078, 39, 25.
EA: interj.: 'well!' 'so!'. *10*: 425.
EL: pers. pron. m.: 'he'. *17*: 39, 25, 4938, 235.
ELLA: pers. pron. f.: 'she, her, it'. *7*: 5078, 425, 39, 25, *13*: 235, *31*: 39, 25, 235, *32*: 5078, 425, 39, 25, 4938.
ELLO: pers. pron. neut.: 'it'. *44*: 425, 25.
ELLOŠ: pers. pron. n. pl.: 'they, them'. *5*: 5078, 425, 25, 4938, 235, *7*: 235, *33*: 5078, *46*: 39, 25, 4938.
EL(L): def. art. m.: 'the'. *1*: 5078, 25, 4938, 235, *3*: 235, *6*: all, *7*: 39, 4938, *et passim.* Before n. f.: *30*: 5078, 425, 39, 4938, *41*: 425, 39, 25, 235.
[EMPAREJAR]: v.: 'to make equal'. *Emparejó 28*: 235.
EMPERO: conj.: 'but'. *45*: 235.
EN: prep.: End-point of movement ('into'): *1*: all, *20*: 4938; location in: *10*: all, *16*: 5078, 425, 39, 25, 4938, *25*: 5078, 25, 4938, 39, 425, *26, 46*: 425, 39, 25, 4938, 235; location on (surface): *14*: 4938, 235; 'upon' (an instrument): *6*: 5078, 39, *13*: all; 'within, inside of'. *10*: 5078, 39, 25, 4938, 235. Expressions of time: *en akel dia 8*: 5078, 425, 4938, *45*: 39, 425, *en qué tiempo 42*: 235. *Kreer en 18*: 5078, 425. (Probably an error for *i*: *32*: 4938.) Certain special uses seem to be attempts to render (or to interpret) the meaning of the Arabic original: *še abansaron en la obidensya 4*: 4938 'hastened to obey', *rregidores en mandamiento 5*: 235 'conveyers of orders', *¿eš a ti en ke kreaš ...? 18*: 4938 'Are you able to believe ...?' *¿en ke eštaš tu de ...? 43*: 25 'What have you to do with ...?'.
ENBYADO: p. ptc.: 'sent'. *45*: 425, 39, 4938.
ENKLINADO: adj.: 'cast down'. *Enklinad-oš 9*: 5078, 425, *-aš 9*: 39.
[ENTENDER]: v.: 'to understand'. *Š-entyende ke* 'it is understood that, it means that' *14, 42*: 4938.
ENTRE: prep.: 'between'. *7*: 5078, 425, 39, 4938.
ESBULUDREANDO: ger.: 'throbbing'. *8*: 235. *L. Yūsuf* 196 *ešbolotere'ar* 'to beat (wings)'; *Alj. T.* J 3 *ešp(o)lodareando* (glossed as 'weeping', but the passage could admit the meaning

'beating, throbbing'). Cf. Prov. *boldrar* 'to smash, knock over, beat', *esboldrar* 'to break', and Cat. *esbal-*, *esboldregar* 'to burst, fall, or crumble down'.

EŠKARESKO: [v. EŠKURESER].

EŠKERESYO: [v. EŠKURESER].

EŠKRUBIRŠE: [v. EŠKUBRIRŠE].

EŠKUBRIRŠE/ESCUBRIRSE: v. refl.: 'to be revealed' [cf. DESKUBRIRŠE]. *Eškubriršе a 36*: 5078, 25, 235, *eškubrirš-a 36*: 4938, *eškrubirše a 36*: 425. *R. Ališ.* 112v *eškᵘrubirše* 'to be lifted' (darkness). *Batallas* Pal. 3226 *eskᵘrubiʸóse.*

[EŠKURESER/ESCURECER]: v.: 'to make dark'. *Eškuresyo 29*: 5078, 39, 235, *eškurasyo 29*: 25, *eškareskó 29*: 4938, *eškeresyo 29*: 435. *Batallas* 37r 2; *Alj. T.* J 13 *eškuresido.*

[EŠMENORAR]: v.: 'to break in small pieces'. *Ešmenoran 2*: 4938.

EŠMENTIR: v.: 'to deny; to declare something to be a lie' [cf. DESMENTIR]. *Ešmentir 12*: 425, *ešmintyo 21*: 5078, 425, 39, 4938. *Alj. T.* J 13; *Batallas* BN 5313; *Vidal* VI, 24.

EŠMINTYENDO: ger.: 'denying'. *12*: 4938.

[EŠPANDIR]: v.: 'to spread' [cf. EŠTENDER, TENDER]. *Ešpandyo 30*: 5078, 425, 39, *ešpandó 30*: 4938. *Batallas* 78v 3.

EŠPLEYT(E): n.: 'provision' [cf. DEŠPLEYTE]. *-Te 33*: 425, 25, 4938, 235, *-t 33*: 5078. *R. Ališ.* 49v *ešpᵉleyt,* 98 *ešpᵉlet* 'contribution of war'; *Vidal* I, 11 *espleitar* 'disfrutar', *F. Arag.* 140, 4 'id.'; Alvar, *T. dial.* On deverbals in *-e* borrowed from Gallo-Rom. see Y. Malkiel, *RLiR,* XXIII (1959), 80-111, & XXIV (1960), 201-253.

[EŠTAR]: v.: 'to be'. *Eštaš 43*: 25, 4938, 235, *-štaš 43*: 425, 39; *estubieron 46*: 235.

EŠTE: demonstr.: 'this' [cf. AKEŠTE]. Adj.: *10*: 4938, 235, *38*: 425, 39, 235. Pron.: *20*: 4938, *26*: 5078.

EŠTO: demonstr. pron. neut.: 'this'. *42*: 4938.

[EŠTENDER]: v.: 'to spread' [cf. EŠPANDIR, TENDER]. *Eštendyo 30*: 25.

EŠTRELLA: n. f.: 'star'. *Eštrellaš 1*: all.

EXEMPLO: n.: 'example' [cf. DEŠ(Š)ENPLO, INŠ(Y)ENPLO]. *26*: 235.

FAŠTA: prep.: 'until' [cf. DAKÍA, HATA]. *33*: 4938.

[FAZER/HAZER]: v.: 'to do, perform': *fizo 20*: 5078, 425, *hizo 20*: 39, 4938; 'to make (i. e., cause to)': *fizo 23*: 5078, 425, 4938, *hizo 23*: 39.

FE: n. f.: 'faith'. *A la fe* 'in faith, indeed' *13*: 235.

FEYTO: p. ptc. [cf. HEČO]. *Feyto a šaber* 'made known' *44*: 425. Arag.: Alvar, *Dial.,* 152.

FIN: n.: 'end' [cf. KABO]. M.: *44*: 4938; f.: *44*: 425, 39, 235.

FIRᶜAWN(A)/FIRAᶜŪN/FIRAON: n. pr. m.: 'Pharaoh'. *17*: all, *18*: 4938, *21*: 5078, 425, 39, *23*: 4938, *26*: 5078, 425, 39, 4938.

FOLLAMYENTA: [v. AFOLLAMYENTO].

FORTUNA: n. f.: 'fate'. *34*: all.

FRAGUAÇION: n.: 'formation'. *27*: 235.

[FRA(G)WAR]: v.: 'to form, fashion'. *Fragwé 27*: 4938, *fragwó 27*: 25, *fragó 27*: 425, 39. *frawó 27*: 5078. *Alj. T.* BN 4955 *f(a)ragu(w)ar,* J 3 *(f)rawar*; *L. Yūsuf* 102 *fᵃrawar*; *Batallas* Pal. 3226 *fᵃragóla.*

[FUNDIRŠE]: v. refl.: 'to sink'. *Še funden 1*: all. *R. Ališ.* 48v *fundir* 'to drown'.

FUYENDO/HUYENDO: ger.: 'fleeing'. *Fu- 22*: 5078, 425, 25, 4938, *hu- 22*: 39.

FWEGO: n. m.: '(hell-)fire'. *34*: 5078, 425, 39, 4938, *39*: 5078, 425, 39, 25, 4938.

FWERTE/FUERTE: adj.: 'strong'. *27*: 5078, 425, 25, 4938, *34*: 4938; *fwerteš 27*: 39.

FWEŠA/FUESA: n. f.: 'tomb'. *Fwešaš 10*: all. *P. Yūçuf* A 46d; *Alj. T.* J 3; *F. Teruel* 289 *fuessa*; *Vidal* IV, 39 id.; *L. Regum* 1. 31 id.; Badía, *Bielsa.*

GANADO: n. m.: 'livestock'. *Ganadoš 33*: 5078, 425, 39, 25, 4938.

GAYATA: n.: 'shepherd's crook'. *22*: 4938. *R. Ališ.* 110v *gayatō, kayatō*; *L. Yūsuf* 7 *gayato*; *Alj. T.* J 3 *gayata, kayata, gayatigo,* BN 5053 *kayato.*

GLORYA: n. f.: 'glory, Paradise' [cf. ALǦANNA(H)]. *34, 41*: 4938.

GRITAR: [v. KRIDAR].

GWEŠO/HUESO: n. m.: 'bone'. *20*: 4938, *gwešoš 2*: 4938, *11*: 425, 39, 25, 4938, *gwašoš 11*: 5078, *huesos 11*: 235. *Alj. T.* J 3 *gu(w)ešo*; *Batallas* Pal. 3226 *güʷeso.*

GYAR/GUIAR: v.: 'to guide'. *Gío 19*: 4938; *gyarte a 19*: 5078, 425, 39, *te gyará 19*: 25, 235.

ǦAHANNAM/CHEHANNAM: n. pr.: 'Hell' (Ar. *jahannam*). *Ǧa- 36*: 5078, 425, 39, 25, 4938; *che-*: *36, 39*: 235. *Alj. T.* J 3.

ǦENT(E): n. f.: 'people'. *-Nt 23, 26*: 5078, *-nte 23*: 425, 39, 25, 235, *26*: 425, 39, *ǧenteš 23*: 4938. *Batallas* 75r 8 *jent.*

ǦUDISYO/ǦWISYO/JUDIÇIO: n. m.: 'Judgment'. *Ǧudi- 42*: 39, 25, 4938, 235, *43*: 39, *44*: 39, 4938, 235, *45*: 235, *ǧwi- 42, 43, 44, 46*: 425. *Batallas* 10v 10 *judiçiʸo*; *Alj. T.* J 3 *ǧudisi(y)ador*; *F. Teruel* 54 *iudicio*; *F. Arag.* 33,4 id.; *Vidal* 2,7 *iuditio.*

[ǦURAR/JURAR]: v.: 'to swear'. *Ǧuró 1*: all.
ǦWISYO: [v. ǦU(D)ISYO].
HABER: [v. ABER].
HATA: prep.: 'until' (Ar. *ḥattā*) [cf. DAKÍA, FASTA]. *33*: 39. *Alj. T.* J 59.
HAZER: [v. FAZER].
HEČO: p. ptc. [cf. FEYTO]. *Hečo a šaber* 'made known' *44*: 39.
HUESO: [v. GWEŠO].
HUMILLADO: adj.: 'humbled' [cf. UMIL(E), UMILDANSA]. *Humilladas 9*: 235.
ḤALĀL: adj.: 'permitted' (Ar. *ḥalāl*). *5*: 5078, 425, 25; *halāl 5*: 4938. *Alj. T.* J 3.
ḤARĀM: adj.: 'forbidden' (Ar. *ḥarām*). *5*: 5078, *ḥaram 5*: 425, 25, *harām 5*: 4938. *Alj. T.* J 3.
ḪALEQADO: adj.: 'created'. *Ḫaleqadoš 10*: 5078, 425. *R. Ališ.* 5v; *Alj. T.* J 13.
ḪALEQAMYENTO/HALECAMIENTO: n.: 'creation'. *27*: 5078, 425, 25, 4938, 235. *Alj. T.* J 41.
ḪALEQAR: v.: 'to create' (Ar. *khalaqa*). *10*: 4938. *R. Ališ*: 80v; *Alj. T.* J 3.
Ī/Y: conj.: 'and' [cf. E]. *1*: 425, 25, 4938, 235; *2, 3, 4, 5*: all, *et passim.*
INŠ(Y)ENPLO: n.: 'example' [cf. DEŠ(Š)ENPLO, EXEMPLO]. *Inš-enplo 26*: 4938, *-yenplo 26*: 425.
[IR(ŠE)]: v.: (refl.): 'to go (away)'. Pret.: *fuese 22*: 235; imper.: *beš 17*: all.
ISRĀFĪL: n. pr. m.: 'Israfil' (the archangel who will blow his trumpet to announce the Judgment Day). *6*: 4938.
JUDIÇIO: [v. ǦUDISYO].
JURAR: [v. ǦURAR].
KABO: n. m.: 'end' [cf. FIN]. *44*: 25.
KAR: conj.: 'for, because'. *26*: 4938. Alvar, *Dial.* 251, *car.*
KARA/CARA: n. f.: 'face'. *14*: 5078, 425, 25, 39, 235.
KARNE: n.: 'flesh'. *20*: 4938.
KAŠA: n.: 'abode'. *39*: 5078, 425, 4938.
KE/QUE: rel. pron.: 'that, which'. *1, 2, 3, 4, 5, 6*: all, *14, 20*: 4938, 425, *27*: 5078, 425, 39, 25, 4938, *34*: 5078, 425, 39, 25, *46*: all. *Lo ke* 'that which' *35*: all.
KE/QUE: conj.: introducing subordinate clause: *6*: 4938, *13*: 5078, 425, 25, 4938, *18*: all, *19*: 4938, *20*: 5078, 39, *24*: 4938, *25*: 25, *35*: 5078, *42*: 4938, *43, 44*: 39, *46*: all. Assertative, before main clause: *16*: 4938, *17*: 5078, 39, 25, 4938, 235, *22*: 4938, *28, 44*: 235, *45*: 39, 25, 4938, *46*: 39, 4938. Before desiderative subj.: *26*: all. *Depweš ke* & subj.: *10*: 39, *11*: 5078, 425, 39, 25; *para ke* & subj.: *19*: 4938, 235 (w. *para* understood, *45*: 425). *Komo ke 46*: 25.
KE/QUE: interrog. pron.: 'what?'. *42*: 235, *43*: all.
[KERER/QUERER]: v.: 'to want'. *Kyere 5*: all, *kyeren 38*: 425. *Kyere, kišo dezir* 'that means, meant' *31, 43*: 39.
KERYENDO: ger.: 'wanting'. *12*: 5078.
KIŠYENDO: ger.: 'wanting'. *12*: 425, 39. *R. Ališ.* 482.18. Alvar, *Dial.* 226, *quisiendo*; Umphrey, id.
[KLAMAR(ŠE)/LLAMAR]: v. (refl.): 'to call; to be called'. *Še klama 16*: 4938, *klamó 16*: 5078, 425, 25, 4938, *llamó 16*: 39, 235.
KLAREDA-D/-T: n. f.: 'brightness'. *-D 29*: 39, 25, *-t 29*: 5078, 425, 4938.
KOMO/COMO: adv.: 'as, like' [cf. COMO interrog.]. *20*: 4938, *46*: all.
KON/CON: prep.: 'with'. *5*: all, *9*: 25, *22*: 5078, 425, 39, 4938, *25*: all, *36*: 5078, 425, 39, 4938, *44*: 425, 39. *Kreer kon* 'to believe in' *18*: 39, 4938, *38*: 5078, 425, 39, 4938 (*kyeren kon 38*: 425).
[KONPONER]: v.: 'to put together'. *Konpušo 28*: 25.
[KONPRENDER/COMPREHENDER]: v.: 'to punish'. *Konprendyo 25*: 39, 25, 4938, 235, *konprišo 25*: 5078, 425. With this same meaning in *R. Ališ.* 100v, *Alj. T.* J 3; the meaning is a translation of Ar. *ākhadha.*
KONTO/KWENTO: n. m.: 'reckoning'. *Kon- 10, 12, 14*: 4938, *35*: 5078, *kwen- 35*: 425. *R. Ališ.* 83 *konto*; *Alj. T.* J 13 id., and *ku(w)ento*; *F. Arag.* 190, 6 *conto.*
KORASON/CORAZON: n.: 'heart'. *Korasoneš 8*: 5078, 425, 39, 25, 4938, *corazones 8*: 235.
KREBANSO: n. m.: 'punishment' [cf. PENA, TORMENTO]. *25*: 4938. *R. Ališ.* 57v *krebantō* 'distress'; *Batallas* 17v 6 *k[e]rebanto* 'aflicción, apuro'; Alvar, *Dial.* 169, *crebanto.* Our form may well be an error for *krebanto* (*krebantar* < *CREPANTĀRE 'to break'; cf. *k[e]rebantado, P. Yúçuf* A 16b).
KREŠTAL: adj. or n.: 'crystal'. *20*: 4938.
KREYENTE/CREYENTE: n. m.: 'believer'. *Kreyenteš 2*: 5078, 425, 25, 235.
[KRE(Y)ER/CREER]: v.: 'to believe'. *Kreyerá 38*: 5078, 4938, *kreerá 37*: 235, *38*: 39, *40*: 235; *kreyaš 18*: 5078, *kreaš 18*: 425, 39, 4938, 235.

[KRIDAR/GRITAR]: v.: 'to cry, shout'. *Kridó 24*: 25, *gritó 24*: 235. *R. Ališ.* 11v *k^{i}rido*; *L. Yūsuf* 21 *k^{i}ridar*; *Alj. T.* J 3 id.; *F. Teruel* 763 *critar*; *F. Arag.* 300, 2 *cridar.* See *DCELC,* II, 791.

KUL(W)EBRA/KULEBRO/QULEBRA: n. m. or f.: 'serpent'. *Kul-ebra 22*: 5078, 39, *-webra 22*: 4938, *-ebro 22*: 425, 4938, *qulebra 22*: 25. *R. Ališ.* 114v *kuluwro*; *L. Yūsuf* 67 *kulebro,* 157 *kullu^{w}ebra*; *Batallas kul-ebro, -u^{w}ebra, -u^{w}ebro.*

KWANDO/QUANDO: adv.: 'when'. *11*: 235, *16*: all, *25*: 5078, 425, 39, 4938, *34*: all, *44*: 4938. Interrog.: *42*: 425, 39, 25, 4938, *43*: 425, 39.

KWANTO/QUANTO: conj. (preceded by *a*): 'as for'. *37*: all, *40*: 39, 25, 4938, 235.

KWAR-ANTA/-ENTA: num.: 'forty'. *-Anta 7*: 5078, 4938, *-enta* 425, 39. Alvar, *Dial.* 211, *quaranta.*

KWENTO: [v. KONTO].

KWERNO: n. m.: 'horn, trumpet' [cf. BOZINA, TRONPA]. *6*: 4938, *34*: 5078, 425, 39, 25.

KYEN/QUIEN: rel. pron.: 'who, whom'. *26, 36, 37, 40*: all, *45*: 425, 25, 4938, 235.

LA: unstr. pers. pron. 3 f. s., d. o.: 'her, it'. *7*: 5078, *20*: 5078, 39, 4938, *30*: 25, 4938, 235, *36*: 4938, *38*: 5078, *46*: 235.

[LANSAR]: v.: 'to throw, cast'. *Lansaba 22*: 4938, *lansó 22*: 5078, 425, 39.

LA(Š): def. art. f., s. & pl.: 'the'. *1, 4, 6, 7*: all, *3*: 5078, 425, 25, 4938, *5*: 4938, *10*: all, *et passim.*

[LEBANTAR]: v.: 'to raise' [cf. ALSAR]. *Lebanta 28*: 4938, *lebantó 28*: 5078, 425.

LE(Š): unstr. pers. pron., 3 s. m. & f., ind. o.: 'him, her, them'. *5*: 4938, *17*: 25, 4938, 235, *18*: all, *19*: 4938, *24*: 4938, 235, *26*: 5078, 425, 39, 4938, *44*: 425, 39, 25, *45*: 4938, *46*: all; elided *-l 35*: 5078.

LLAMAR: [v. KLAMAR(ŠE)].

LLEGADO: [v. PLEGADO].

LLEGAR: [v. PLEGAR].

LO: def. art., neut. s.: 'the'. *5*: 5078, 425, 25, 4938. Followed by *ke,* rel. 'that which': *5*: 235, *26*: 5078, 425, 39, 4938, *35*: all.

LONBRAMYENTO: n.: 'mentioning, naming' [cf. NONBRAMYENTO]. *43*: 4938. *R. Ališ.* 15 'reputation'; *Alj. T.* J 13; *P. Yúçuf* A 67d *lonb^{a}rar*; *R. Ališ.* 68 id.; *L. Yūsuf* 271 id.

LO(Š): unstr. pers. pron., 3 m. s. & pl., d. o.: 'him, it, them'. *14*: 39, 235, *16*: all, *21*: 5078, 425, 39, 25, *25*: all, *27*: 5078, 425, 39, 25, 4938, *28*: 25, 235, *32*: all, *45*: 425, 39, *46*: 425, 39, 25, 4938.

LOŠ: def. art. m. pl.: 'the' [v. EL]. *2, 3, 4, 5*: all, *6*: 235, *9*: 5078, 4938, *et passim.*

LWEGO: adv. 'afterward' [cf. APREŠ, DEPWEŠ]. *14*: 5078, 425, 4938.

MALO: adj.: 'evil'. *Maloš 36*: all.

MANDA-MYENTO/-MIENTO/MANDEMYENTO: n. m.: 'command'. *Manda- 5*: 235, *18*: 5078, 425, 39, 25, *21*: 5078, 425, 39, 25, 4938; *mande- 18*: 25.

MANNANA: n. f.: 'morning' [cf. MANNANADA]. *46*: 425, 39, 25, 235.

MANNANADA: n. f.: 'morning' [cf. MANNANA]. *46*: 4938. Borao; Pardo Asso 'primeras horas de la mañana'.

MANO: n. f.: 'hand'. *20*: 5078, 425, 39, 25, 4938.

MAR: n.: 'sea'. M.: *3*: 235; f.: *3*: 5078, 425, 25, 4938, *25*: 5078, 425, 39, 25, 4938. On the gender see O. K. Lundberg, *HR,* I (1933), 309-318, and Y. Malkiel, *Lg.,* XXVII (1951), 485-518.

MAŠ: adv.: 'more, most'. *12*: 4938, *24*: 5078, 425, 39, 25, 4938, *27*: all.

MAYOR: adj.: 'greatest'. *20, 34*: all.

MENUDO: adj.: 'small'. *Menudoš 11*: 5078, 235.

[METER]: v.: 'to put' [cf. PONER(ŠE)]. *Mišo 32*: 5078.

MILAGRO/MIRAGLO: n. m.: 'miracle'. *Mil- 20*: 5078, 425, 39, 25, *mir- 20*: 4938. *L. Yūsuf* 151 *miraglo*; *Alj. T.* J 13 id.; *Vidal* IX, 60 id.

MINTIRA: n.: 'falsehood'. *24*: 4938. *L. Yūsuf* 32.

MINTROŠ(O): adj.: 'false'. *-Ošo 12*: 5078, *-oša 12*: 425, 4938, *-oš 12*: 49. *L. Yūsuf* 18; *Alj. T.* J 3; *F. Teruel* 713 *mintrosa mientre. Batallas* T 18 *ment^{o}roso,* 49r 12 *mintiroso.*

MIRAGLO: [v. MILAGRO].

MIŠO: [v. METER].

MONEŠT(EY)ADOR: n.: 'warner, admonisher'. *-Eyador 45*: 4938, *-ador 45*: 235. *Alj. T.* J 3 *monešt-ar, -ear*; *Batallas* 14r 10 *monestador.*

MONTE: n. m.: 'mountain'. *16*: 4938, *monteš 32*: all.

MUÇE: [v. MŪSĀ].

MUČO: adv.: 'much'. *42*: 4938, *43*: 39.

MUḤAMMAD/MUHAMED: n. pr. m.: 'Mohammed' [cf. ANNABĪ]. *15*: 25, 4938, 235, *42*: 39, 25, 235, *43*: 4938, 235, *44*: 235, *45*: 4938.

MUNDO: n. m.: 'world'. *10, 38*: all, *25*: 5078, 425, 25, 4938, 235, *46*: 425, 39, 25, 4938, 235.
MŪSĀ/MUÇE: n. pr. m.: 'Moses'. *15*: all, *17*: 5078, 425, 39, 25, *20, 22*: 5078, 425, 39, 4938.
MWERTE: n. f.: 'death'. *33*: 5078, 425, 39, 4938.
MWERTO: adj.: 'dead'. *Mwertoš 10*: 39.
MYEDO: n.: 'fear' [cf. TEMOR]. *8*: 4938, *19*: 5078, 425, 4938, *26*: 5078, 425, 39, 4938, *40*: 5078, 425, 39, 25, 4938, *45*: 425, 39, 4938.
NO: adv. of negation: 'no, not'. *12*: 5078, 425, 39, 25, 4938, *13*: 5078, 425, 4938, *26, 38*: 5078, 425, 39, 4938, *37*: 235, *44*: 425, *45*: 425, 39, 25, 4938, *46*: all.
NOČE/NOCHE: n. f.: 'night' [cf. NWEY(TE)]. *29*: 39, 25, 4938, 235.
NONBRA-MYENTO/-MIENTO: n.: 'mentioning, naming' [cf. LONBRAMYENTO]. 43: 39, 25, 235.
NONBRE: n.: 'name'. *16*: 5078, 425, 39.
NWEBAMENT(E): adv.: 'anew'. *-Nt 10*: 5078, 4938, *-nte* 425.
NWEB(E): num.: 'nine'. *-Ebe 20*: 425, 39, 4938, *-eb 20*: 5078.
NWEY(TE): n.: 'night' [cf. NOČE]. *-Ey 29*: 5078, *-eyte 29*: 425. *Alj. T.* J 3 *nwey*.
O: conj.: 'or'. *27*: all, *42*: 4938, *46*: all.
OBIDENSYA/OBEDENSYA/OBIDIENÇIA: n. f.: 'obedience'. *Obid-ensya 4*: 4938, 25, *19*: 4938, *-iençia 4*: 235, *obedensya 4*: 5078, 425. *R. Ališ.* 45 *obidençiʸa*; *L. Yūsuf* 97 id., 89 *obedensiʸa*. All these variants are documented by Y. Malkiel, *UCPL,* I (1945), 123-124.
OBRA: n.: 'work, action'. *Obraš 35*: 5078, 425.
OBRADO: p. ptc.: 'done'. *35*: all.
OǦO: n. m.: 'eye' [cf. WELLO]. *Oǧoš 9, 20*: 4938.
ORA: n. f.: 'hour'. *46*: 425, 235; *la ora* (adv.) 'then' *12*: 25. *P. Yúçuf* A 61a *la ora* adv.; *L. Yūsuf* 52 id.; *Alj. T.* J 3 id.; Alvar, *T. dial.* id.; Umphrey id.
[ORDENAR]: v.: 'to ordain'. *Ordena 5*: 4938.
OTRO: adj.: 'other'. *7*: 5078, 39, 4938, *25*: 5078, 25, 4938, *38*: 5078, 425, 39, 4938, 235; *otra 25*: 39, 235; *otra beš* 'again' *20*: 4938.
PARA(D): prep.: 'for'. *Para 10*: 4938, *26*: 39, 25, 4938, 235, *32*: 4938, 39, *36*: 4938, 235; *para ke* 'in order that' *19*: 4938, *33*: 25; *parad 45*: 25. *Alj. T.* BN 5053 *parad*; *F. Teruel* 181 *porad*.
PARADA: n. f.: 'standing' [cf. PARAMYENTO, PORPARAMYENTO]. *40*: 235.
PARAMYENTO: n. m.: 'standing' [cf. PARADA, PORPARAMYENTO]. *40*: 4938.
[PARESER(ŠE)/PAREÇERSE]: v. (refl.): 'to seem'. *Paresen 46*: 425, *paresera 46*: 39, 25, *še leš paresera 46*: 4938, *pareçerseles a 46*: 235.
[PARTIR(ŠE)]: v. (refl.): 'to leave, set out'. *Parten 1*: 425, 25, 4938, 235, *še parten 1*: 5078.
PASTO: n.: 'pasturage'. *Pastos 31*: 235.
PEDRIKADOR: n.: 'preacher' [cf. PREIKADOR]. *45*: 425, 25, 4938. *Alj. T.* J 3 *pedrikar*; *Batallas* 114v 8 *pedrikaba*; Umphrey.
PENA: n. f.: 'punishment' [cf. KREBANSO, TORMENTO]. *25*: 5078, 425, 39, 25, 4938, *36*: 5078, 425, 39, 5948, *45*: 425, 39.
PERDIÇION: n.: 'loss'. *12*: 235.
PERDIDO: adj.: 'lost'. *Perdida 12*: 25, 4938.
PERŠONA: n. f.: 'person' [cf. PREŠONA]. *35, 40*: 39, 25, 235.
PILAR: n.: 'pillar'. *Pilareš 27*: 5078, 425, 39, 4938, *28*: 25.
PLANO: adj.: 'flat'. *Plana 14*: 4938.
[PLAZER]: v.: 'to please'. *Plaze 5*: 4938.
PLEGADO/LLEGADO: p. ptc.: 'reached'. *Ple- 15*: 4938, *18*: 5078, 425, 25; *lle- 18*: 39.
PLEGAR/LLEGAR: v.: 'to arrive'. *Plegar 23*: 5078, 425, 25, 4938, *42*: 425, 4938; *llegar 23*: 39; possibly trans., 'to bring together': *llegó 23*: 235; n. m. 'arrival' *44*: 25.
[PODER]: v.: 'to be able'. *Pwede 12*: 5078, 425, 39, 25, 4938.
PODRIDO: adj.: 'rotten'. *Podridoš 11*: 5078, 425, 39, 25, 4938.
[PONER(ŠE)]: v. (refl.): 'to put' [cf. METER]. 'To set', intrans.: *še ponen 1*: 4938; *ponia 20*: 4938, *pušo 32*: 425, 39, 25, 4938.
PONYENT(E)/PONIENTE: n. m.: 'West'. *-Yent 1*: 5078, 4938, *-yente 1*: 425, 25, 235.
POR: prep. 'by': *1, 2, 3, 4, 5*: all; 'across, through': *3*: all; 'concerning': *42*: all; 'for the purpose of': *45*: 39.
PORKE: conj. 'in order that': *33*: 5078, 425, *45*: 39; 'because': *43*: 39.
PORPARAMYENTO: n. m.: 'standing' [cf. PARADA, PARAMYENTO]. *40*: 5078, 39, 25. *R. Ališ.* 32v *porparar* 'to show', 84 'to prepare'; *Batallas* 67v 2 *porparar* 'presentar'.
PREIKADOR: n.: 'preacher' [cf. PEDRIKADOR]. *45*: 39.
PREŠONA: n. f.: 'person' [cf. PERŠONA]. *35*: 5078, 4938, *40*: 5078, 425, 4938, *R. Ališ.* (frequent); *L. Yūsuf* 11; *Alj. T.* J 13; *Batallas* 1r 2. On the prefixes *per-, pre-, pro-* see Y. Malkiel, *RPh,* III (1949-50), 27-72.
PRIMERO: adj.: 'first'. *6*: 4938, *primera* 5078, 425, 39.

PROMETIMYENTO: n. m.: 'promise'. *40*: 425. Probably an error for *porparamyento*.
PWEŠ/PUES: conj.: 'well'. *13*: 5078, 39, 25, *27*: 25, 4938, *34*: 39, 25, 235, *43*: 425, 39; 'then, therefore': *19*: 5078, 425, 39, 25; *a kwanto ... pweš* (Ar. *ammā ... fa*): *39, 41*: all.
PYEDRA: n. f.: 'stone'. *20*: 4938.
QUANDO: [v. KWANDO].
QUANTO: [v. KWANTO].
QUE: [v. KE].
QUERER: [v. KERER].
QUIEN: [v. KYEN].
QULEBRA: [v. KUL(W)EBRA].
[RRANKAR]: v.: 'to pull, pluck out' [cf. ARRANKAR]. *Rrankan 2*: 425. *Batallas* 112v 7.
[RRAPAR]: v.: 'to steal'. *Rrapan 20*: 4938. *Batallas* 35v 6. For this meaning see *Dicc. Aut.* s. v. *rapar*.
RRATO: n. m.: '(brief) period of time'. *46*: 425, 39, 25.
RREBIBKADO/RREBIBCADO: adj.: 'resurrected'. *Rrebibkad-oš 10*: 39, *14*: 235, *-aš 14*: 25. *Batallas* 103v 12.
RREBIBKAR: v.: 'to resurrect'. *10*: 25. *R. Ališ.* 43; *Alj. T.* J 3.
RREDRA: [v. RRIDRA].
RREFIRMAMYENTO: n.: 'strengthening' [cf. AFIRMAMYENTO]. *32*: 5078, 425, 39, 25, 4938; 'establishment' *42*: 425, 39, 25, 4938. *Batallas* Pal. 3226 *rrefirmarse*.
RREGIDOR: n. m.: 'ruler'. *Rregidores 5*: 235.
[RREĞIR]: v.: 'to rule'. *Rriğe 5*: all.
RREKONTAMYENTO: n. m.: 'account, story' [cf. YSTORIA]. *15*: 5078, 425, 39, 25, 4938. *R. Ališ.*; *L. Yūsuf 326*; *Alj. T.* BN 5053; *Vidal* II, 13 *recontamiento*.
[RREKORDARŠE]: v. refl.: 'to recall' [cf. ACORDARSE]. *Še rrekordará 35*: 5078, 39, 25, 4938.
RRELUNBRANTE: pres. ptc. & adj.: 'shining'. *20*: 5078, 425, 39, 25, 4938. *Alj. T.* E1880.
[RRESEBIR]: v.: 'to receive'. *Rresibe 45*: 425, 39.
RRESPLANDOR: n.: 'brightness'. *29*: 235.
RRETIEMBLANTE: pres. ptc. & adj.: 'shaking' [cf. TINBLANTE, TREMULANTE]. *7*: 235.
RRETORNARŠE: v. refl.: 'to return' [cf. BOLBER(SE), TORNAR(ŠE)]. *Še rretornará 7*: 4938.
[RRETRONAR]: v.: 'to resound'. *Rretronarán 6*: 235.
RRETRONIDO: n. m.: 'blast' [cf. SOFLIDO, ŠOFLO, TOKADA, TOKAMYENTO, TOKIDO]. *Rretronidos 6*: 235. On the suffix *-ido* see s. v. SOFLIDO.
RRIDRA/RR(Y)EDRA: adv.: 'back' [cf. SAGA]. *Rri- 22*: 39, 25, *rre- 22*: 4938, *rrye- 22*: 4938 (all followed by [*a*] *saga*). *R. Ališ.* 86v *rredrar* 'to withdraw'; *Alj. T.* BN 4955 id.; *Batallas* 15r 11 *rredrado* 'alejado'; *Vidal* I, 42 *fiador de riedra*. On RETRŌ and its semantic evolution see J. Corominas, *RPh*, I (1947-48), 23-31.
RRYEDRA: [v. RRIDRA].
ŠABER: v.: 'to know'. *44*: 425, 39; *šabed 13*: 5078, 425, 25, 4938; n. 'knowledge' *44*: 425, 39, 235.
SAGA: adv.: 'behind, back' [cf. RRIDRA]. *22*: 5078, 425, 39, 25, 4938. *P. Yúçuf* A 16a; *R. Ališ.* 35; *L. Yūsuf* 16; *Alj. T.* J 3; *Vidal* I, 56; *F. Arag.* 153,6; *Libro Verde*.
SAGERO: adj.: 'last' [cf. SAGA]. *34*: 39, 4938, *sagera 34*: 5078, 425. *P. Yúçuf* B 16a; *R. Ališ.* 113; *Alj. T.* J 3; *Batallas* 107v 10.
[ŠAKAR/SACAR]: v.: 'to take out'. *Šaka 29*: 39, *31*: 5078, 39; *šakaba 20*: 5078, 425, 39, 4938; *šakó 29*: 5078, 425, 25, 4938, 235, *31*: 425, 25, 4938, 235.
[ŠALBAR(ŠE?)]: v. (refl.?): 'to preserve; be preserved?'. *Šalboše 24*: 4938, possibly an error for *šalbo šea*.
ŠALLYENT(E)/SALIENTE: n. m.: 'East'. *-Yent 1*: 5078, 4938, *-yente 1*: 425, 25, 235.
ŠANTO: adj.: 'holy'. *16*: 5078, 425, 39, 25, 4938; *san*[*c?*]*to 16*: 235.
ŠE: unstr. refl. pron. *6*: 5078, 39, 25, 4938, *14*: 4938; elided, *š- 42*: 4938. All used impersonally.
ŠEGIR(ŠE)/ŠIGIRŠE/SEGUIR: v. (refl.): 'to follow'. *40*: 5078, 425, 39, 25, 4938; *še šegirá 7*: 25; *še šigirá 7*: 39; *seguirá 7*: 235.
ŠEGUNDO: adj.: 'second'. *Šegunda 7*: 5078, 425, 39, 25, 4938.
ŠEMEĞANTE: indef. pron.: (followed by *de*) 'the likes of' [cf. ŠENBLANTE]. *26*: 4938.
ŠENBLANTE: indef. pron.: (followed by *de*) 'the likes of' [cf. ŠEMEĞANTE]. *26*: 5078, 425, 39. *Alj. T.* J 3 *šenb*(*a*)*lante de* 'the same as'.
ŠENNOR/SEÑOR: n. m.: 'Lord' (of God); *16*: all, *18*: 39, 25, *19, 24, 40*: all, *44*: 25, 235.
ŠENO: n.: 'bosom'. *20*: 5078, 425, 39, 4938.
ŠER/ŠEYER: v.: 'to be'. Inf.: *šer 10*: 425, 39, 25, 235, *12*: 425, 39, 25, *42*: 425, 25, 4938, *34*: 425, 39, *šeyer 10*: 5078, 4938, *11*: 4938, *12*: 5078, 4938, *42, 44*: 4938; pres. ind.: *šo 24*: 5078, 425, 4938, *šoy 24*: 39, 25, 235, *ereš 45*: 25, 235, *eš 18*: 4938, 235, *26*: 5078,

39: 39, *41*: 39, 25, *44*: all, *šoeš 27*: 4938, *šoyš 27*: 425, 39, 25, 235, *šos 27*: 5078; imperf.: *era 16*: 5078, 425, 39, *20, 24*: 4938, *š-era* (refl.) *20*: 4938; pret.: *fušte 45*: 425, 39, *fwe 20*: 5078, 425, 39, *44*: 425, 39, *fweron 46*: 425, 39, 25, 4938; fut.: *šera 12*: 5078, 425, 39, 25, 4938, *13*: all, *14*: 4938, *34*: 5078, 425, 39, 25, 4938, *37*: 5078, 425, 39, 25, *39*: 5078, 425, 25, 4938, 235, *41*: 425, 4938, 235, *42*: 39, 235, *46*: 25, *šeran 9*: 5078, 425, *14*: 5078, 425, 4938; cond.: *seria 12*: 235; pres. subj.: *šia 33*: 5078, *šea 33*: 425, 25, *šeamoš 10*: 39, *11*: 425, 39, 25, 235, *šeyamoš 11*: 5078. Impersonal ('to occur, take place'): *šera 7*: 5078, 425.

ŠEY(Š)SYENTOŠ: num.: 'six hundred'. *Šeyš- 28*: 39, *šey- 28*: 425.

ŠIGIRŠE: [v. ŠEGIR(ŠE)].

ŠIN: [v. ŠINŠE].

ŠINEŠ: [v. ŠINŠE].

ŠINO: conj.: (preceded by *no*) 'no more than, nothing but'. *13*: 5078, 425, 39, 4938, *45*: 425, 39, 25, 4938, *46*: all.

ŠINŠE/ŠINEŠ/ŠIN: prep.: 'without'. *Šinše 27*: 5078, 425, 25, *šineš* (*de*) *27*: 4938, *šin 27*: 39. *P. Yúçuf* B 215d *šinše*; *R. Ališ.* 92v id.; *L. Yūsuf* 63 id.; *Alj. T.* J 3 id. The *šinše* variant seems confined to Aljamiado, while *sines* is found in Aragonese as well: *Vidal* I, 70; *F. Arag.* 37,7; *L. Regum* 12.27; Alvar, *T. dial.*

SINSYENTOŠ: num.: 'five hundred'. *28*: 5078, 4938. Alvar, *Dial.* 211, *cincientos.*

ŠOBE-/ŠOBI-RANO: adj.: 'high, exalted' [cf. ALTO]. *Šobe- 24*: 39, 25, 235, *šobi- 24*: 5078, 425, 4938. *Alj. T.* BN 4944 *šobirano.*

ŠOBRE: prep.: 'on, over'. *14*: 5078, 425, 39, 25, *30*: 5078, 425, 39, 4938, *38*: 235.

SOFLIDO: n. m.: 'blast' [cf. RRETRONIDO, ŠOFLO, TOKADA, TOKAMYENTO, TOKIDO]. *13*: 235. On the sound-suffix *-ido* see J. R. Craddock and E. S. Georges, *RPh,* XVII (1963-64), 87-107.

ŠOFLO: n. m.: 'blast' [cf. RRETRONIDO, SOFLIDO, TOKADA, TOKAMYENTO, TOKIDO]. *34*: 5078, 425, 39, 25, 4938. *Alj. T.* J 13 *šoflar*; *Batallas* Pal. 3226 *suflo.*

ŠOL: n. m.: 'sun'. *29*: all.

ŠOLO: adv.: 'only'. *13*: 39, 25, 235.

ŠOŠTENI-MYENTO/-MIENTO: n.: 'support'. *27*: 25, 235.

ŠOŠYEGO: n.: 'rest, resting-place' [cf. AŠENTAMYENTO, ASITIADA]. *39*: 5078, 425, 39, 25, *41*: 425, 39, 25. See Y. Malkiel, *PhQ,* XXIII (1944), 297-306, and W. Geiger and P. Smith, *PhQ,* XLIII (1964), 112-122.

SUBḪĀNAHU: Ar. formula: 'praise to Him' (after the name of God). *5, 13*: 4938.

ŠU(Š): poss. adj. m. & f., s. & pl.: 'his, her, their'. *9*: 39, 25, 235, *16*: all, *20*: 5078, 425, 39, 25, 4938, *22*: 4938, *23*: 4938, 235, *et passim.*

SYELO/ÇIELO: n. m.: 'sky, Heaven'. *27*: all.

TAN: adv.: 'as'. *20*: 4938.

TARDE: n. f.: 'afternoon, evening'. *46*: all.

TE: [v. TU].

[TEMER]: v.: 'to fear'. *Teme* (pres. ind.) *26*: 25, 235, *45*: 25, *temera 26*: 5078, 39, *40*: 235, *45*: 425, 39, *tema 45*: 235, *temas 19*: 235, *teme* (imper.) *19*: 235.

TEMEROŠO: adj.: 'fearful' [cf. AMEDRESIDO]. *Temerošaš 9*: 39, 25.

TEMOR: n.: 'fear' [cf. MYEDO]. *26*: 4938.

TENBLANTE: [v. TINBLANTE].

[TENDER]: v.: 'to spread' [cf. EŠPANDIR, EŠTENDER]. *Tendio 30*: 235.

TĪ: [v. TU].

TIEMPO: n.: 'time'. *42*: 235.

TIERRA: [v. TYERRA].

TINBLANTE/TENBLANTE: pres. ptc. & adj.: 'trembling' [cf. RRETIEMBLANTE, TREMULANTE]. *Tin-blanteš 8*: 5078, 25, *ten- 8*: 425, 39.

TODO: adj.: 'all'. *Todoš 20*: 4938, *todaš 14*: 25, *23*: 4938.

TOKADA: n. f.: 'note, blast' [cf. RRETRONIDO, SOFLIDO, ŠOFLO, TOKAMYENTO, TOKIDO]. *6*: 5078, 425, 39, *7*: 39, 25, 4938.

TOKADO: p. ptc.: 'played, sounded'. *13*: 25.

TOKAMYENTO: n. m.: 'note, blast' [cf. RRETRONIDO, SOFLIDO, ŠOFLO, TOKADA, TOKIDO]. *7*: 5078, 425, 39, *13*: 5078, 425, 39, 25, 4938.

[TOKARŠE]: v. refl.: 'to be played, sounded' (instrument). *Še tokará 6*: 5078, 425, 39, 25, 4938.

TOKIDO: n. m.: 'note, blast' [cf. RRETRONIDO, SOFLIDO, ŠOFLO, TOKADA, TOKAMYENTO]. *6, 7*: 4938. On the suffix *-ido* see s. v. SOFLIDO.

[TOMAR]: v.: 'to take'. *Tomarán 35*: 5078, 425.

TORMENTO: n. m.: 'punishment, torment' [cf. KREBANSO, PENA]. *25*: 235.

TORNADA: n. f.: 'return' [cf. TORNADO n., TORNAMYENTO]. *12*: 425, 25, 4938, 235.
TORNADO: n. m.: 'return' [cf. TORNADA, TORNAMYENTO]. *12*: 5078, 39.
TORNADO: p. ptc. *Tornadoš* & adj. 'restored' *10*: 5078, 425, 235; *tornadoš a rrebibkar* (*ḫaleqar*) 'resurrected (created) anew' *10*: 25, 4938.
TORNAMYENTO: n. m.: 'return' [cf. TORNADA, TORNADO n.]. *12*: 5078, 425, 39, 4938. *R. Ališ.* 9v 'circling'.
[TORNAR(ŠE)]: v. (refl.): 'to turn (into), return' [cf. BOLBER(ŠE), RRETORNARŠE]. *Torna 12*: 4938, *tornan 12*: 425, *tornaba 20*: 4938, *tornabaše 22*: 4938, *tornoše 22*: 5078, 425, 4938.
TRAS: prep. (followed by *de*): 'after' [cf. APREŠ, DEPWEŠ]. *7*: 235.
[TRA(Y)ER]: v.: 'to bring'. *Trayrán 34*: 5078, 39, 4938, *traeran 34*: 425.
TREMULANTE: pres. ptc. & adj.: 'trembling' [cf. RRETIEMBLANTE, TINBLANTE]. *Tremulanteš 8*: 4938. *R. Ališ.* 3v *t^eremular*; *L. Yūsuf t^eremolar*; *Batallas* 46r 4 id.
TRONPA: n. f.: 'trumpet' [cf. BOZINA, KWERNO]. *34*: 4938.
TTOGUE: [v. ṬUWĀ].
TU: unstr. pers. pron., 2 s. m. & f.: 'you'. *43*: all, *45*: 25, 4938, 235; o. of prep.: *18*: 235, *45*: 425, 39.
TU: poss. adj., 2 s. m. & f.: 'your'. *18*: 39, 25, *19*: all, *44*: 25, 235.
  TE: unstr. pers. pron., 2 s. m. & f.: 'you'. D. o.: *19*: 5078, 39, 25, 4938, 235; ind. o.: *15*: 5078, 39, 25, 4938, 235, *18*: 5078, 39, 25, (refl.) 25, *42*: all.
  TĪ: str. pers. pron., 2 s. m. & f.: 'you'. *18*: 4938.
ṬŪRI SĪNĀ: n. pr.: 'Mount Sinai' (Ar. *Ṭūr Sīnā'*). *14*: 4938.
ṬUWĀ/TTOGUE: n. pr.: (place name, unidentified). *16*: all.
TYERRA/TIERRA: n. f.: 'earth'. *14, 30*: all, *31*: 5078, 425, 39, 4938.
UMIL(E): adj.: 'humble' [cf. HUMILLADO]. *Umileš 9*: 5078, 425. *Vidal* IX, 60 *húmil.* Singular forms *umil* and *umile* are both documented in Old Spanish and it cannot be determined which was meant here.
UMILDANSA: n.: 'humility'. *9*: 25. *Alj. T.* J 3. On the *-ança* suffix see Y. Malkiel, *UCPL* I: 4 (1945), 41-188.
UN: indef. art. m. s.: 'a, an'. *22*: 4938, *46*: 39, 25. Possibly the num. 'one': *7*: 5078, 425, 39, 4938, *13*: all.
  UNA: indef. art., f. s.: 'a, an'. *20*: 4938. Possibly the num. 'one': *46*: 425, 4938, 235.
UNO: num.: 'one'. *20*: 5078, 425, 39.
VAXILLO: [v. BAŠILLO].
VENIR: [v. BENIR].
VEOS: [v. BEOŠ].
VER: [v. BER].
VIDA: [v. BIDA].
VIVO: adj.: 'alive'. *Vivos 10*: 235.
VISTA: [v. BIŠTA].
VN: [v. UN].
VOLBER: [v. BOLBER(ŠE)].
VOSOTROS: [v. BOŠOTROŠ].
VOZ: n. f.: 'voice'. *17*: 235.
VOZINA: [v. BOZINA].
VUESTRO: [v. BWEŠTRO].
WELLO: n. m.: 'eye' [cf. OČO]. *Welloš 9*: 5078. *Alj. T.* J 13 *gu(w)elo, welo*; Alvar, *Dial.* 151, *güello.*
Y: [v. I].
YA: adv.: 'already'. *15*: 5078, 425, 39, 25, 235, *18*: 5078, 425, 39, 4938.
YĀ/YE; vocative particle: 'o!' (Ar. *yā*). *15*: 25, 235, *18*: 4938, *42*: 39, 25, 235, *43*: 4938, 235, *44*: 235, *45*: 4938. *Alj. T.* J 3, *L. Yūsuf* 4, *R. Ališ.* (freq.).
YERBA: n.: 'grass'. *Yerbaš 31*: 5078, 425, 39, 25, 4938.
YO: unstr. pers. pron., 1 s.: 'I'. *19*: 4938, *24*: all.
YSTORIA: n. f.: 'story' [cf. RREKONTAMYENTO]. *15*: 235.

VI. PHOTOGRAPHS OF THE TEXTS

1 : BN 5078, 23v-24r.

2: BN 5078, 24v-25r.

3: BN 5078, 25v-26r.

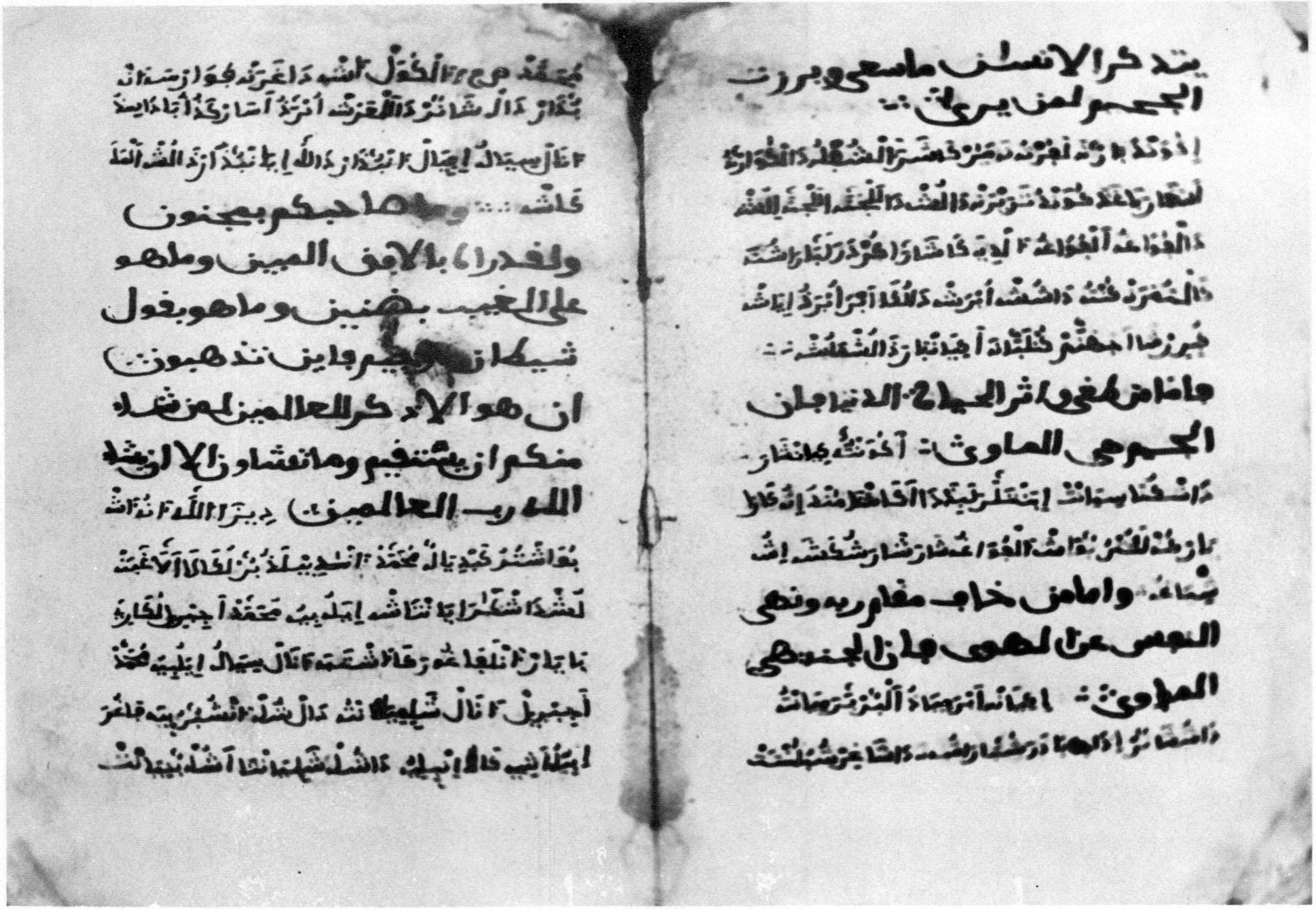

4 : BN 5078, 26v-27r.

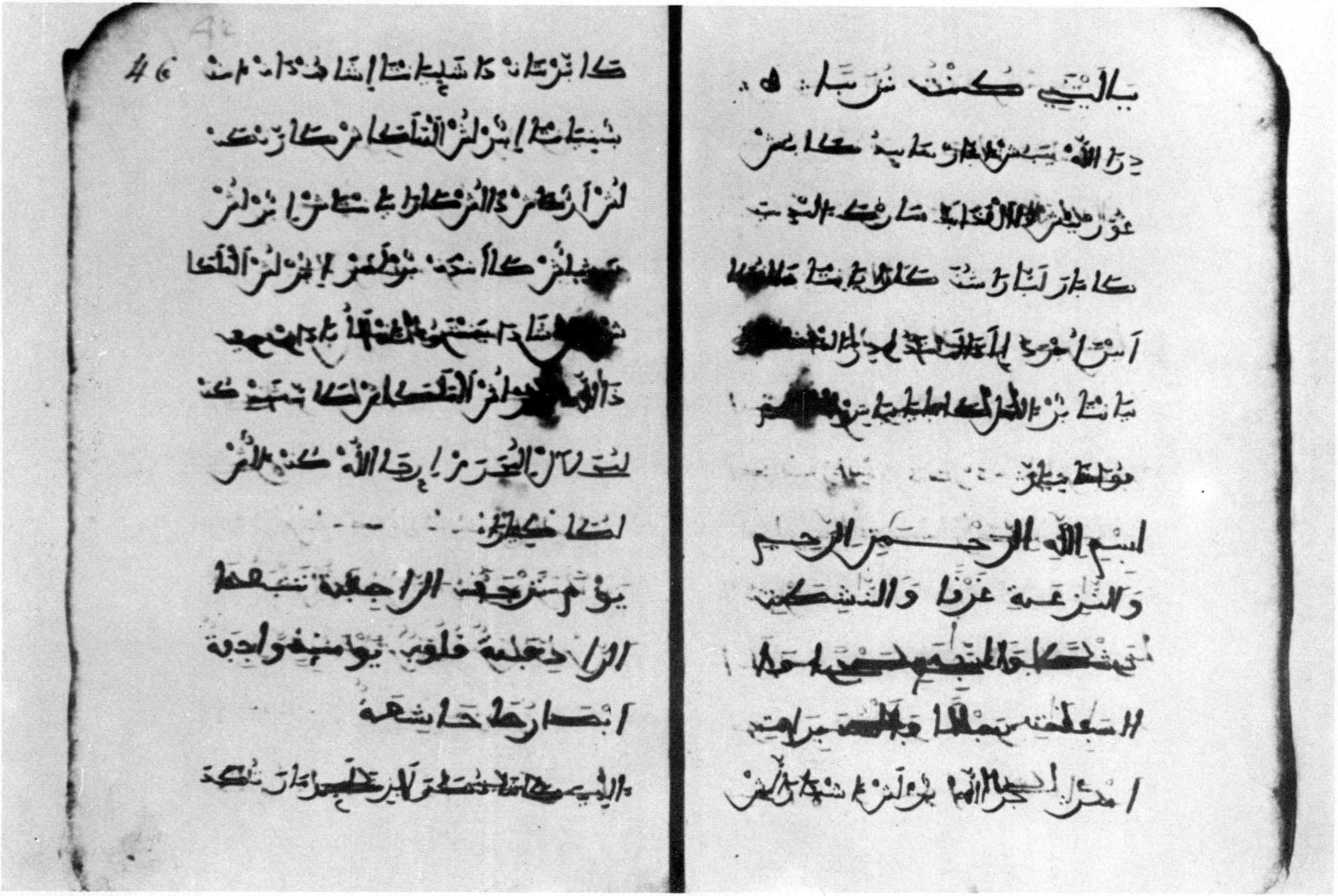

5: P 425, 45v-46r.

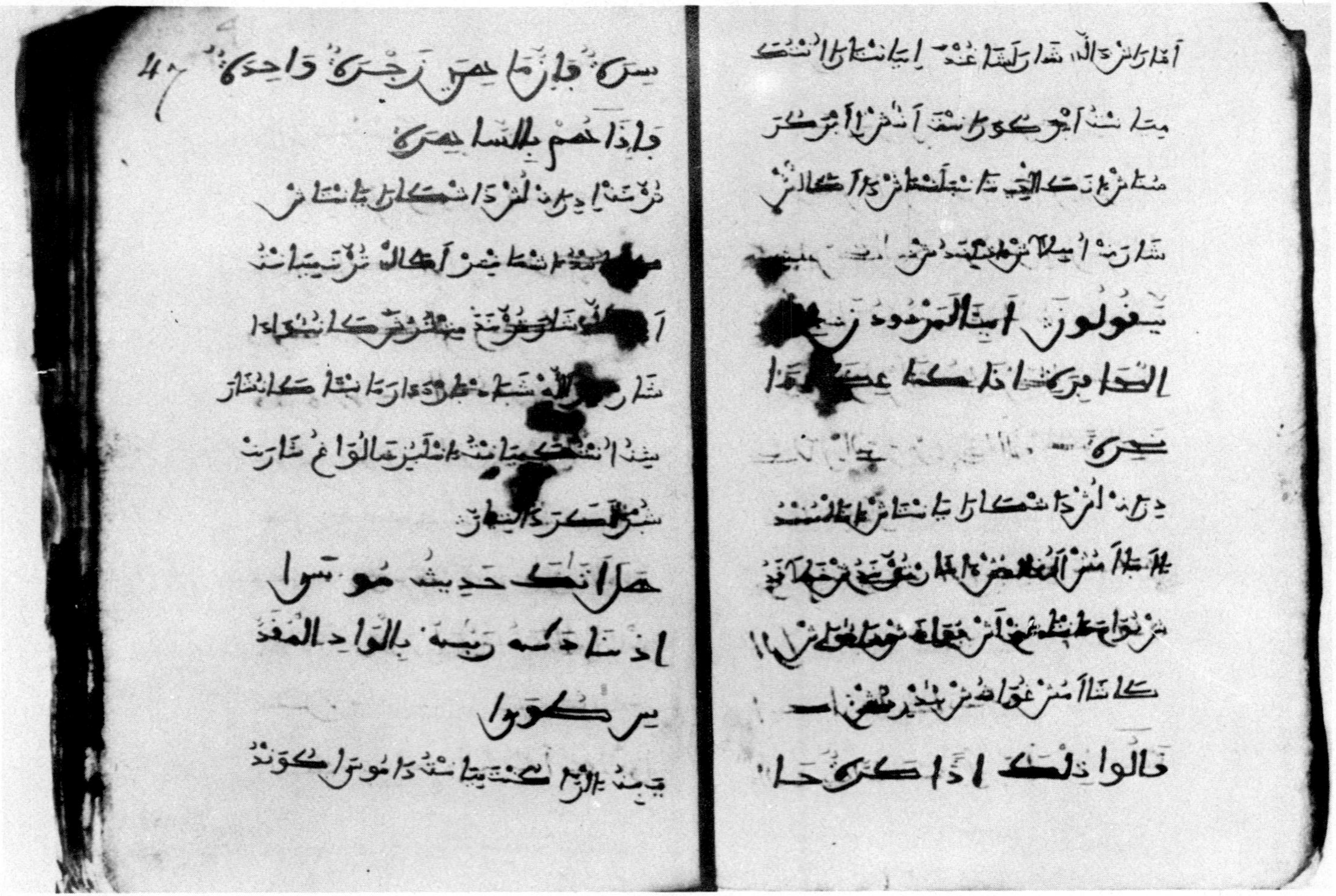

6: P 425, 46v-47r.

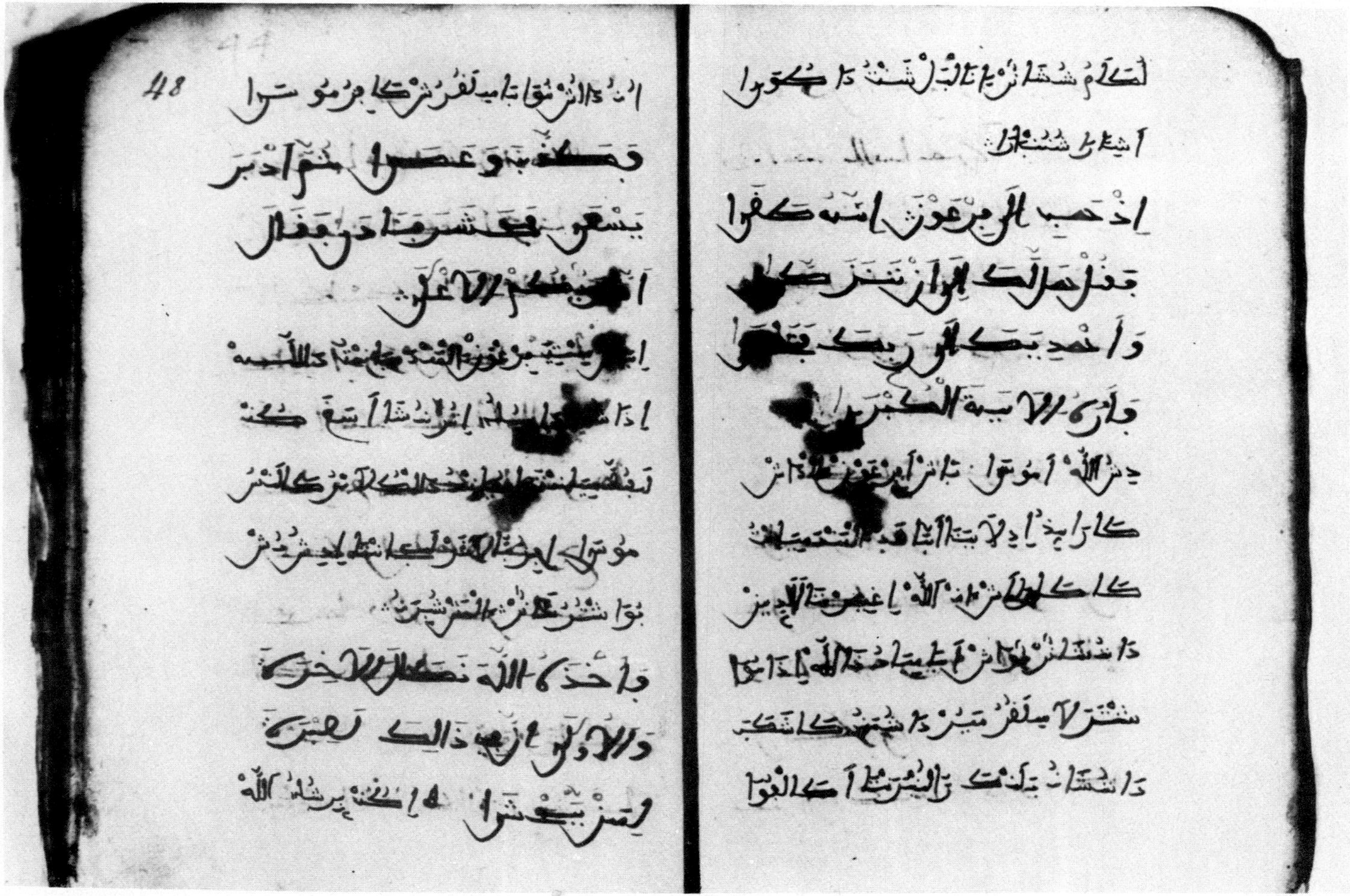

7: P 425, 47v-48r.

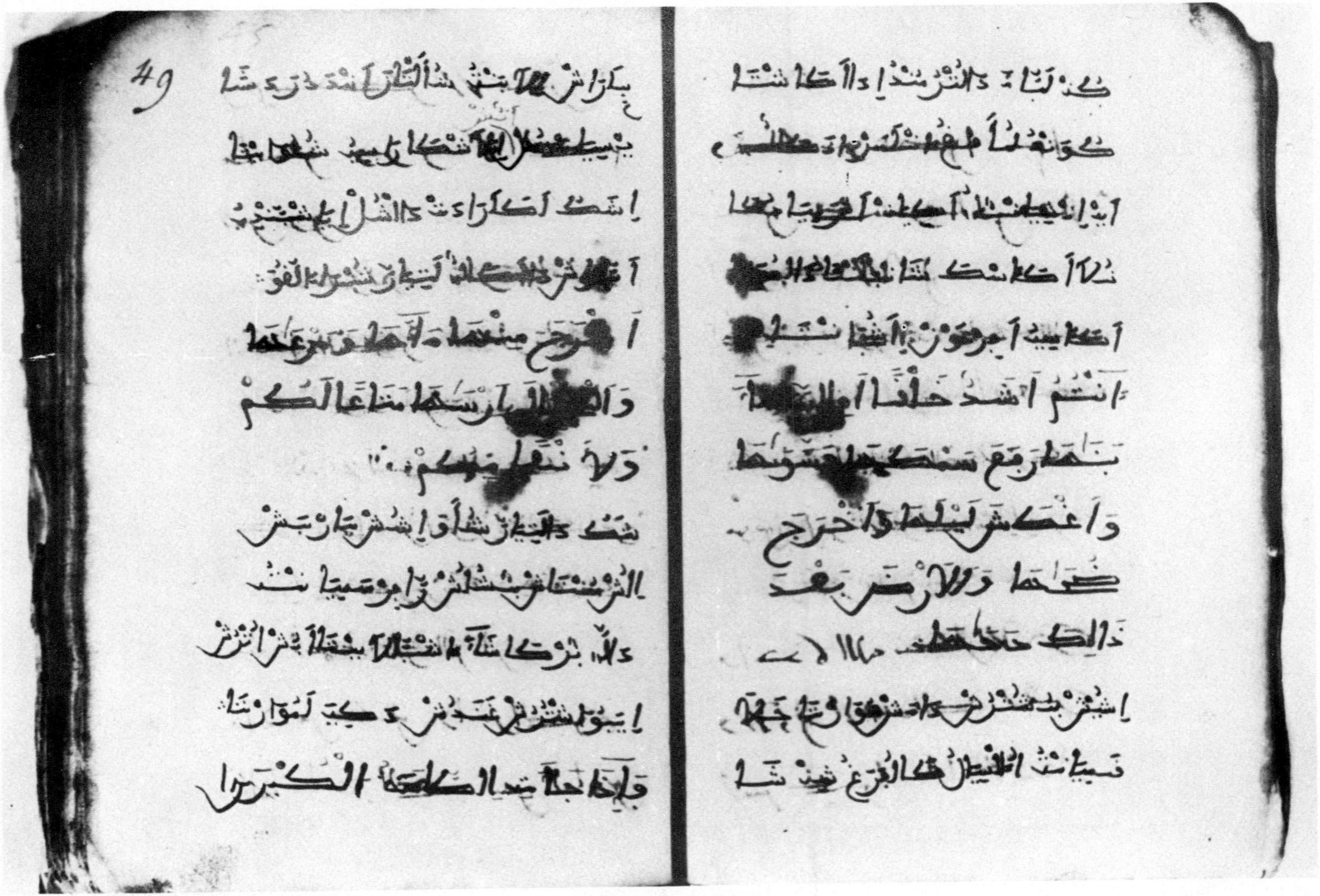

8: P 425, 48v-49r.

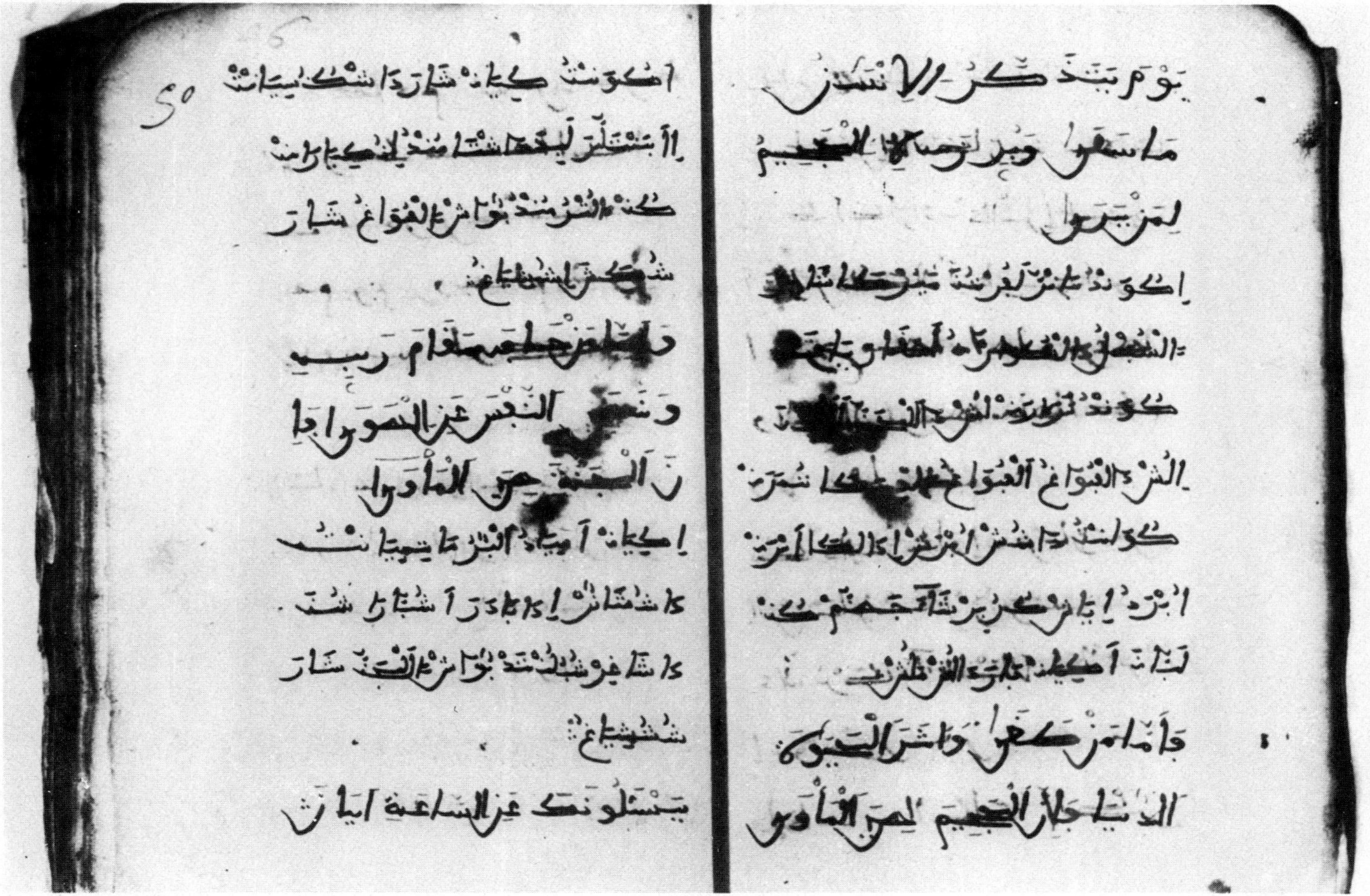

9 : P 425, 49v-50r.

مرسلها فيم انت من ذكرها
الى ربك منتهاها انما
انت منذر من يخشاها كا
نهم يوم يرونها لم يلبثوا
الا عشية او ضحاها

[illegible]

[illegible]

بسم الله الرحمن الرحيم
عبس وتولى ان جاءه الاعمى
وما يدريك لعله يزكى
او يذكر فتنفعه الذكرى

[illegible]

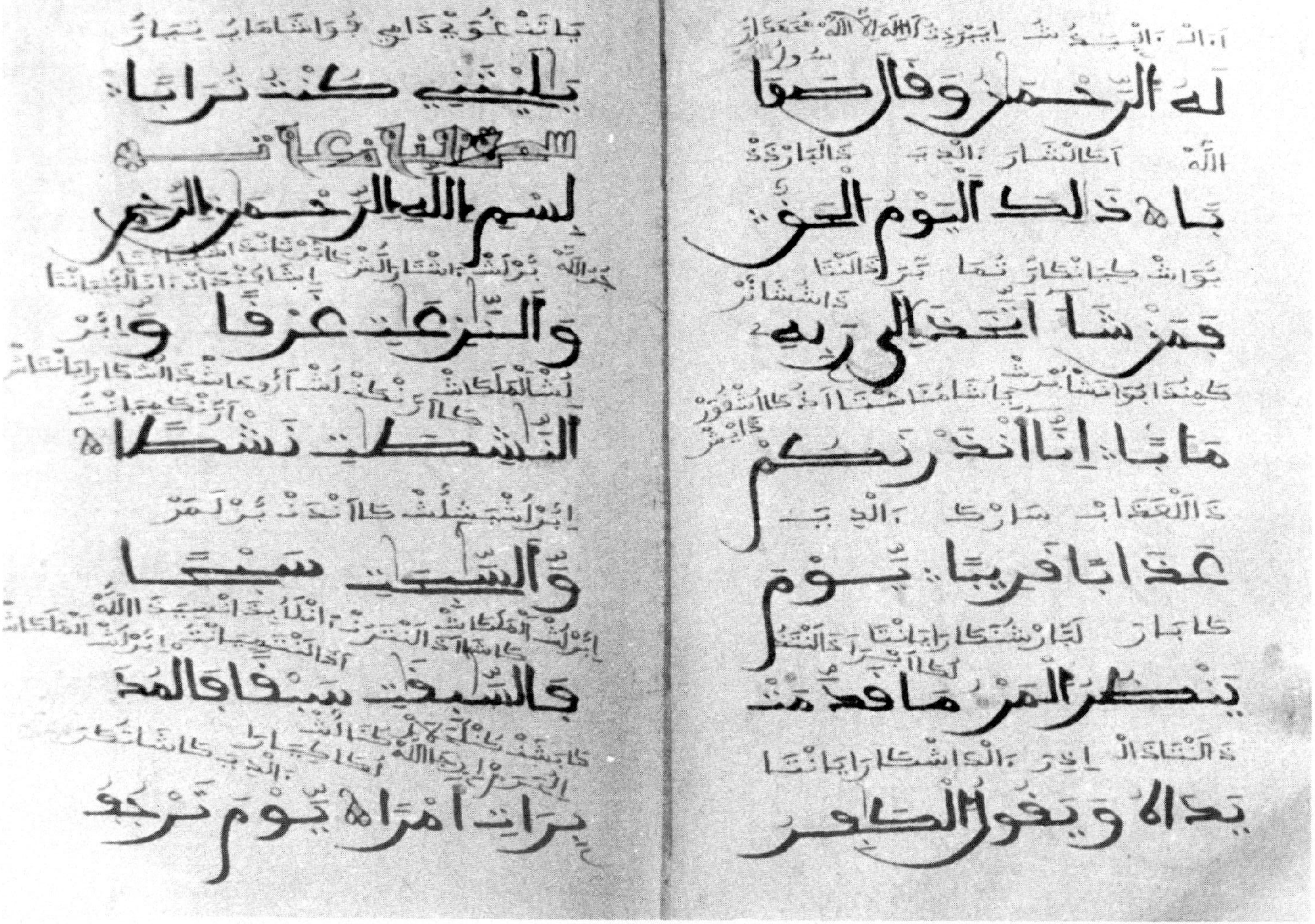

11 : J 25, 37 a-b.

12: J 25, 38 a-b.

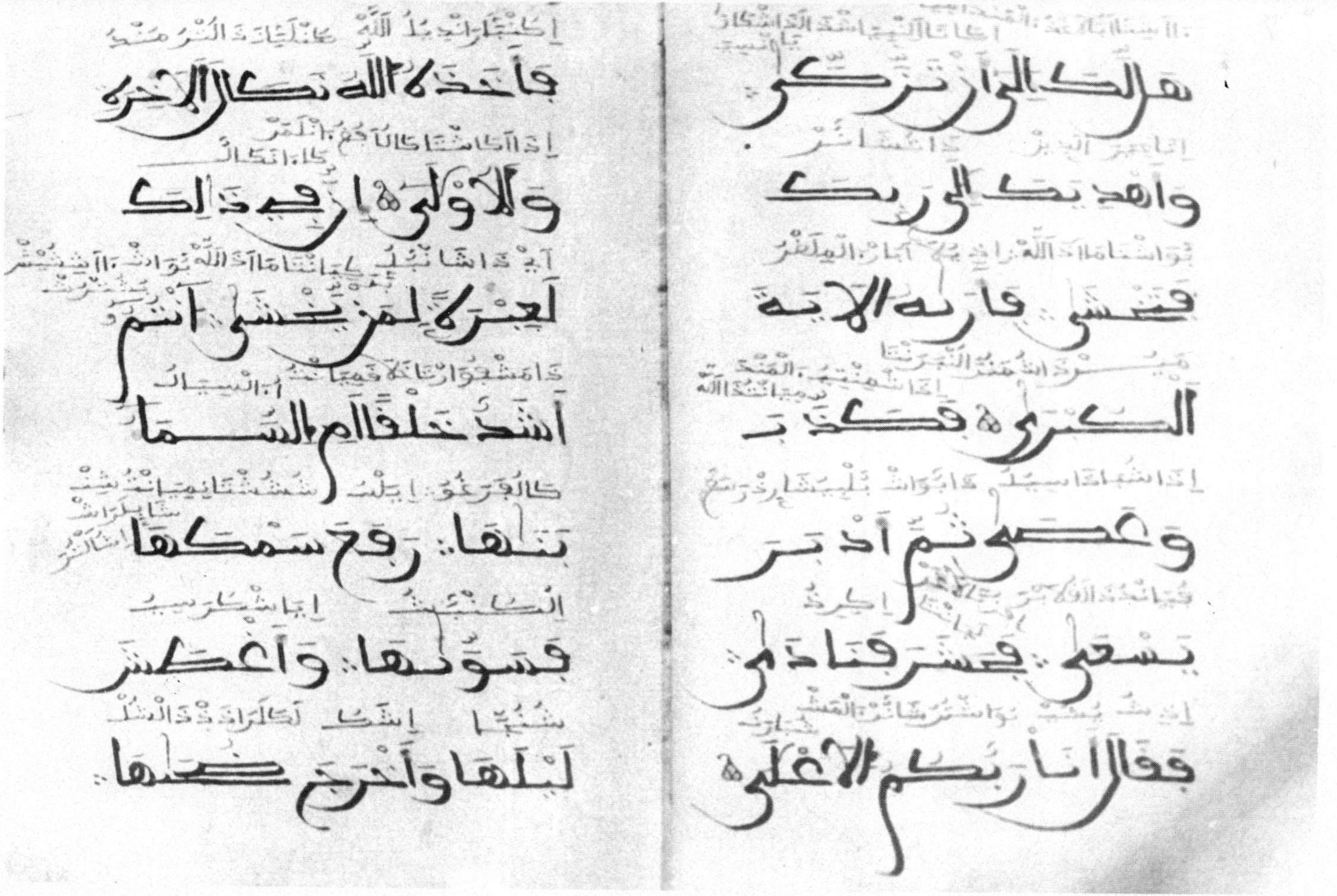

13: J 25, 39 a-b.

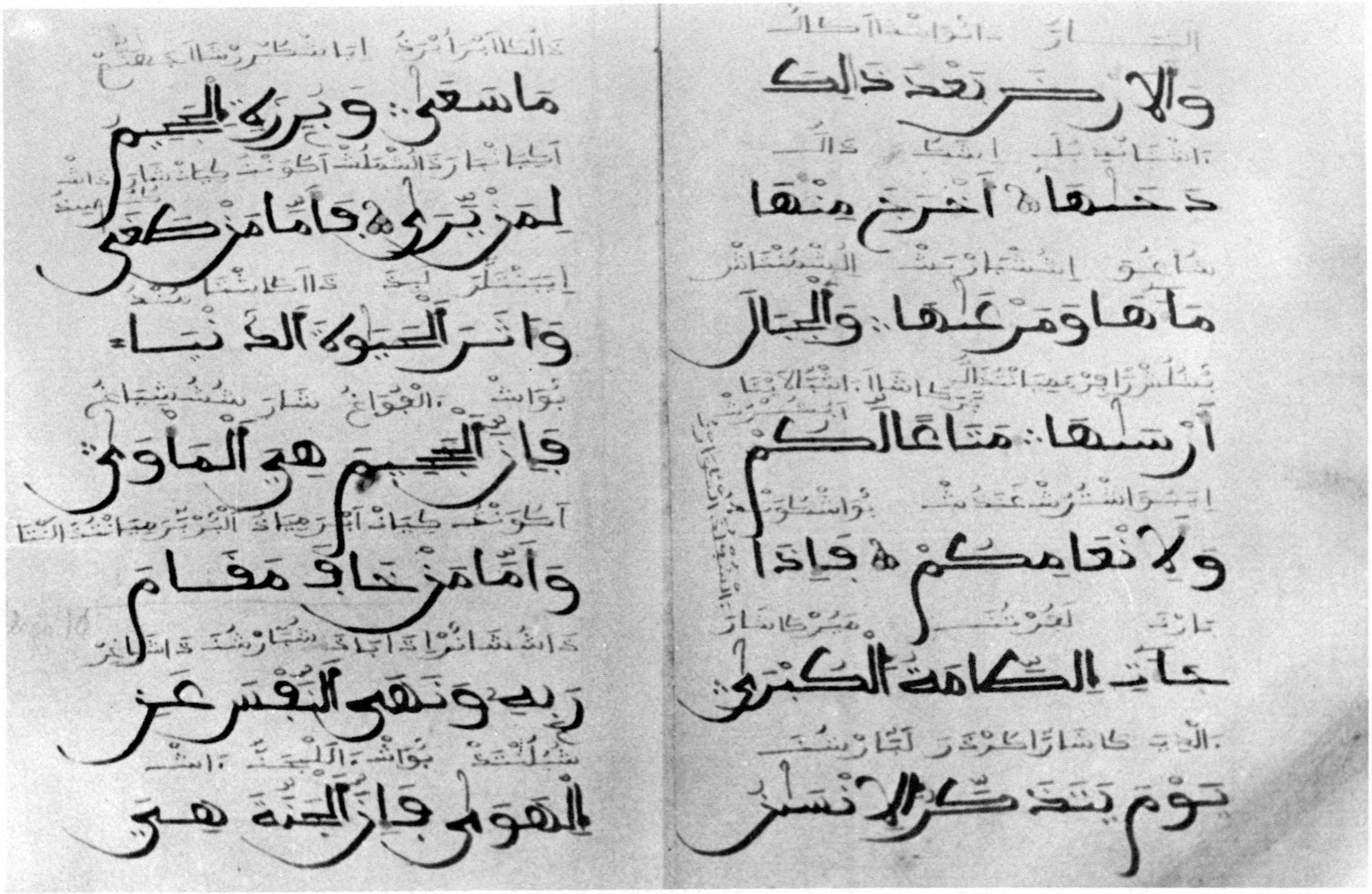

14: J 25, 40 a-b.

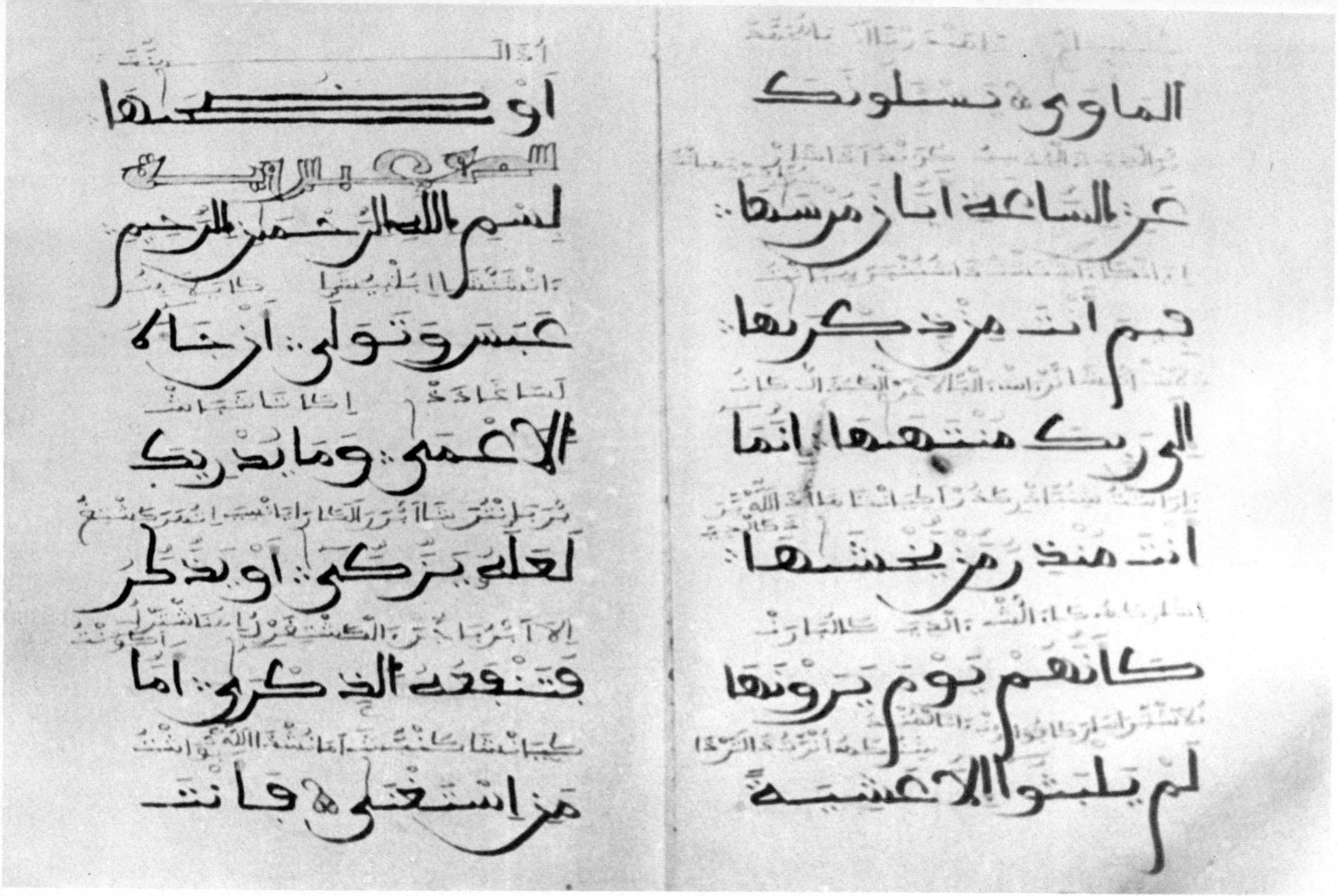
المأوى يسئلونك
عن الساعة أيان مرسىها
فيم أنت من ذكرىها
إلى ربك منتهىها إنما
أنت منذر من يخشىها
كأنهم يوم يرونها
لم يلبثوا إلا عشية
أو ضحىها
بسم الله الرحمن الرحيم
عبس وتولى أن جاءه
الأعمى وما يدريك
لعله يزكى أو يذكر
فتنفعه الذكرى أما
من استغنى فأنت

15: J 25, 41 a-b.

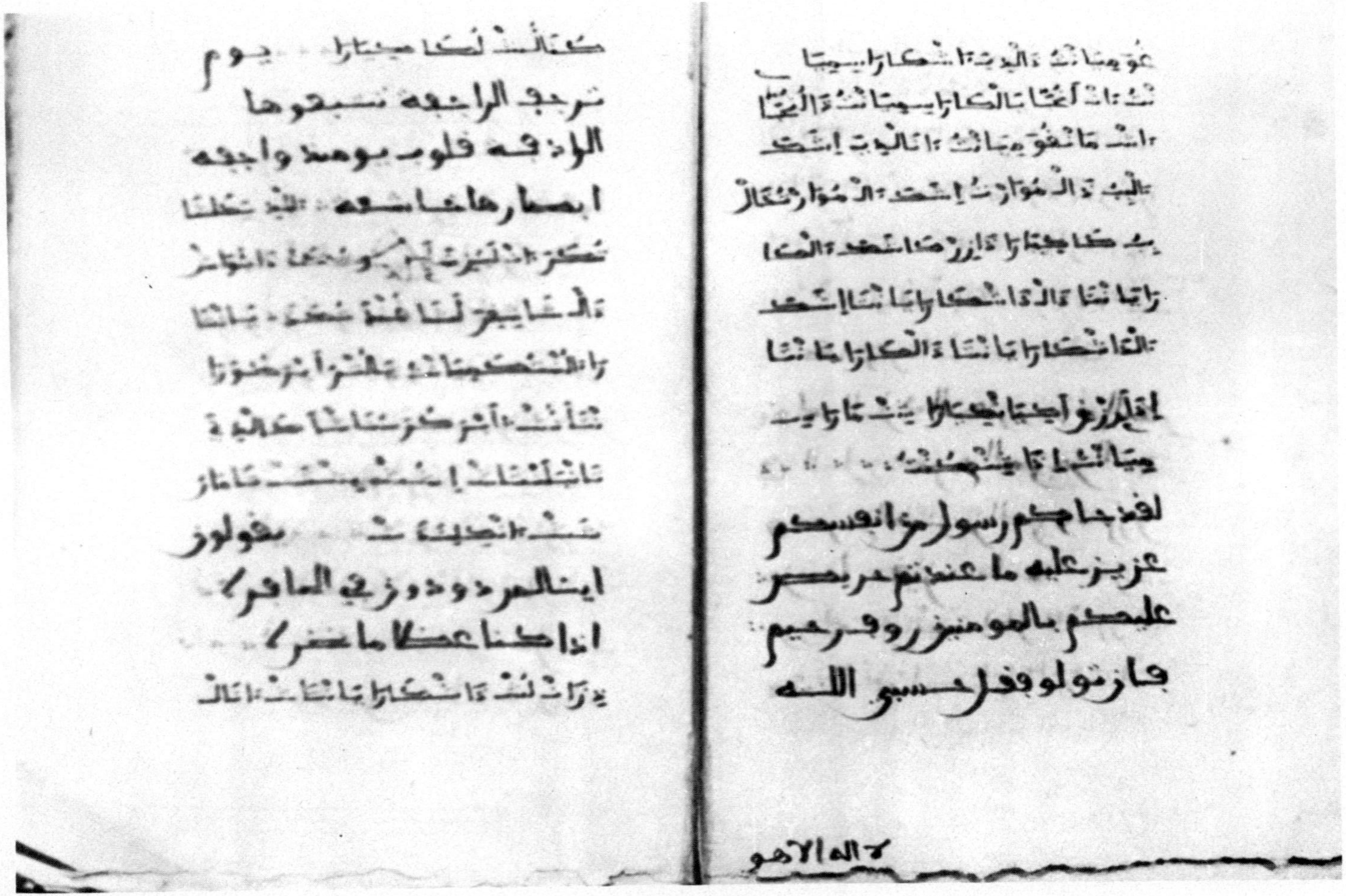

16: J 39, 97v-98r.

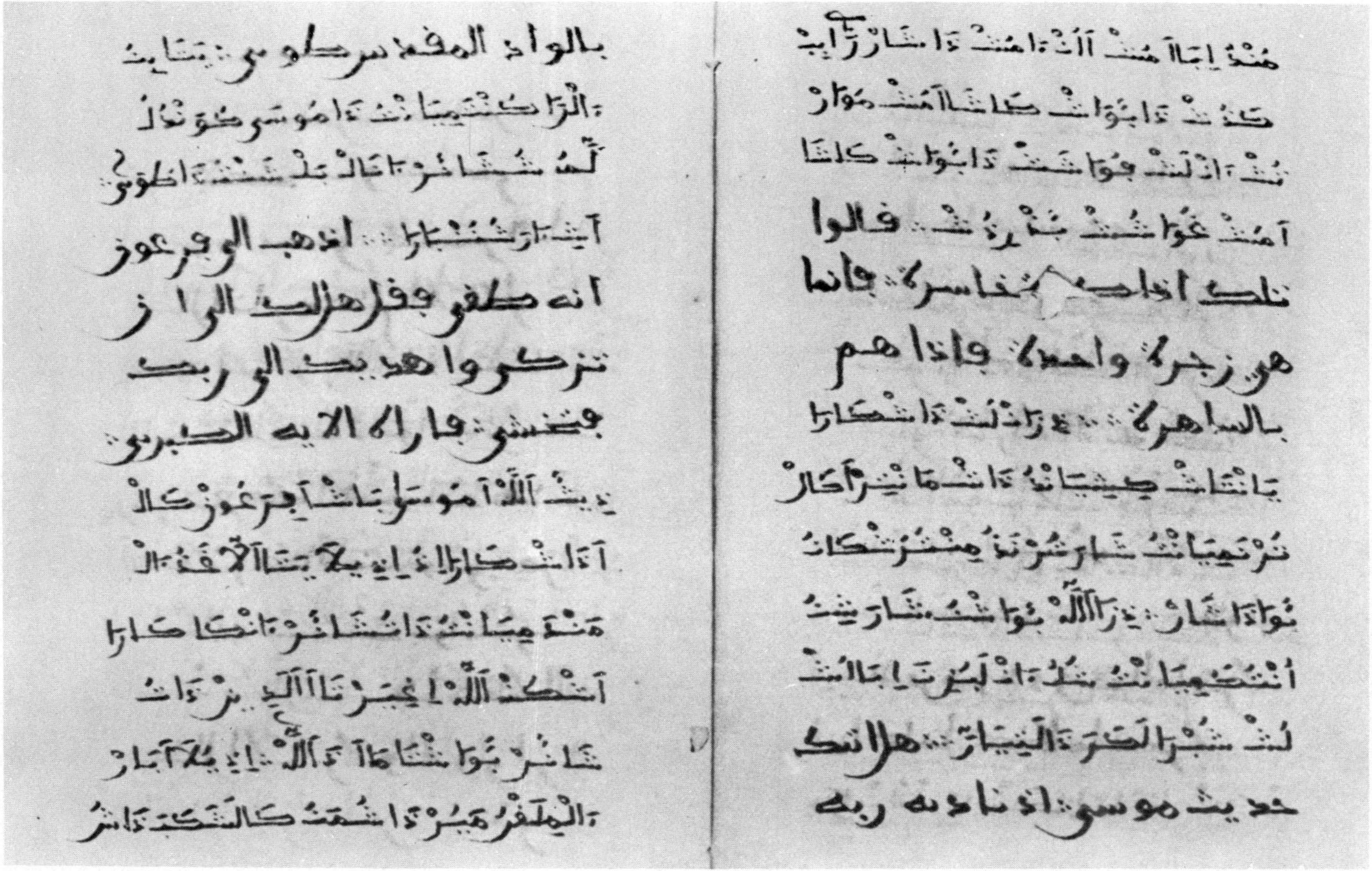

17 : J 39, 98v-99r.

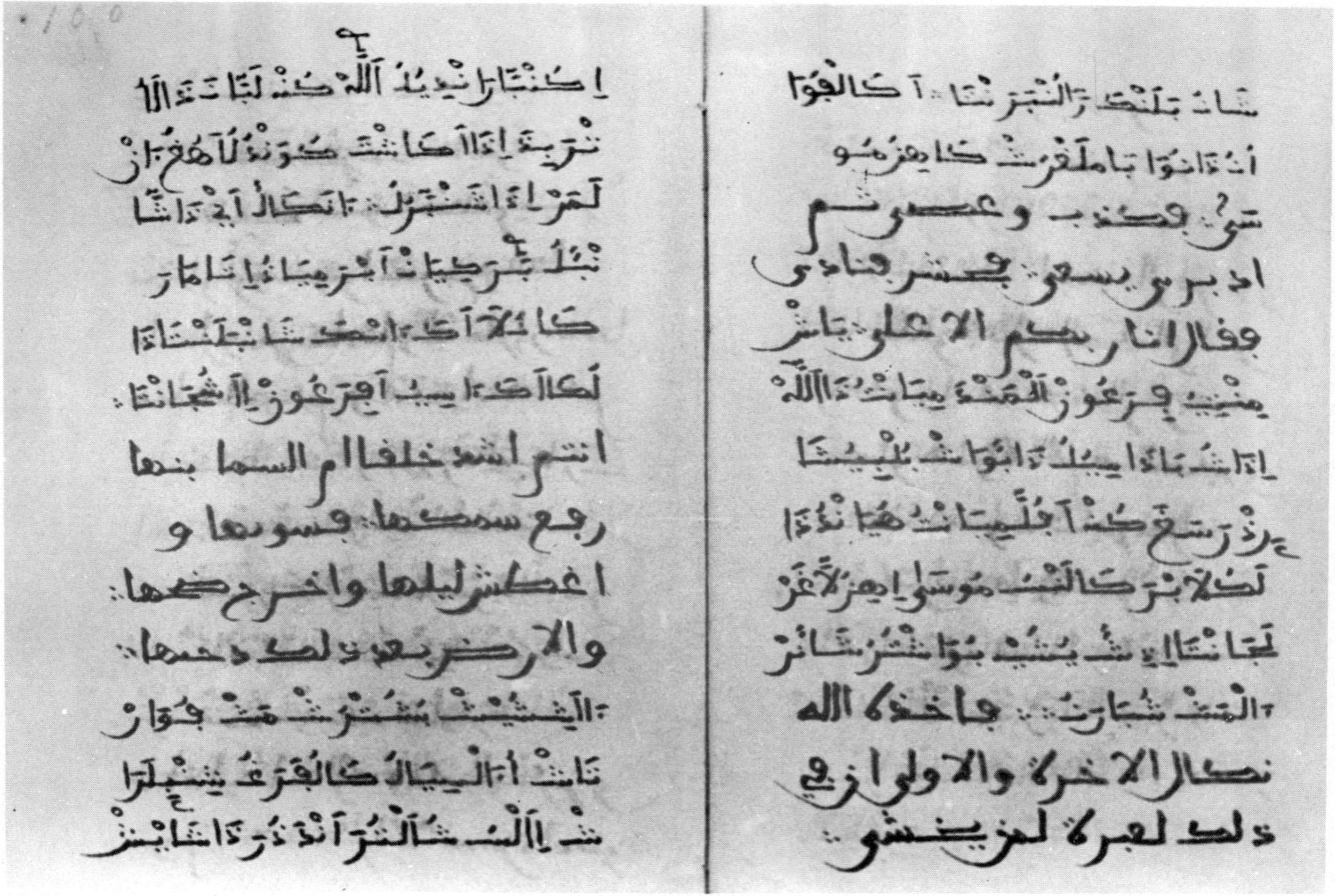

18 : J 39, 99v-100r.

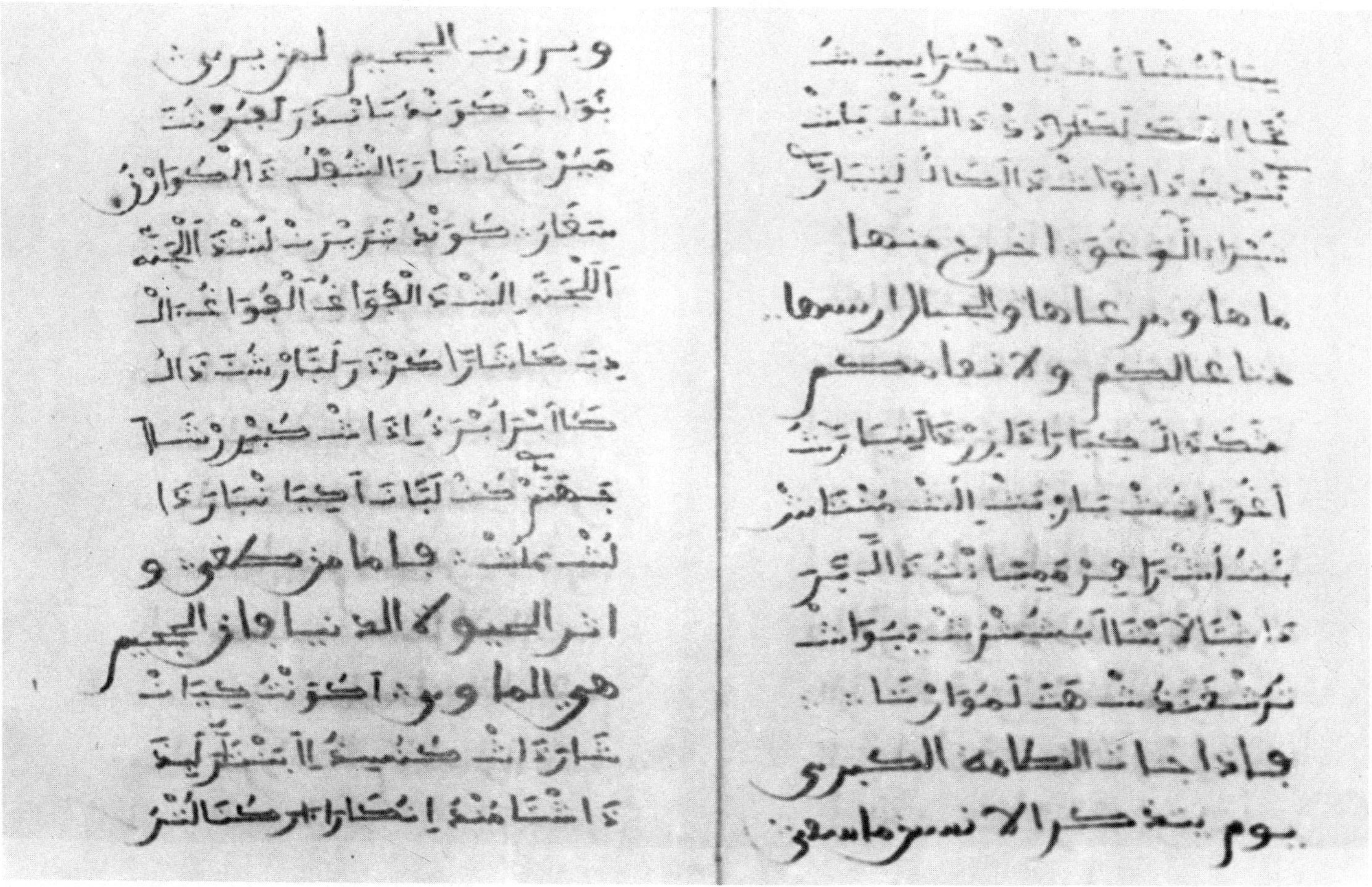

19: J 39, 100v-101r.

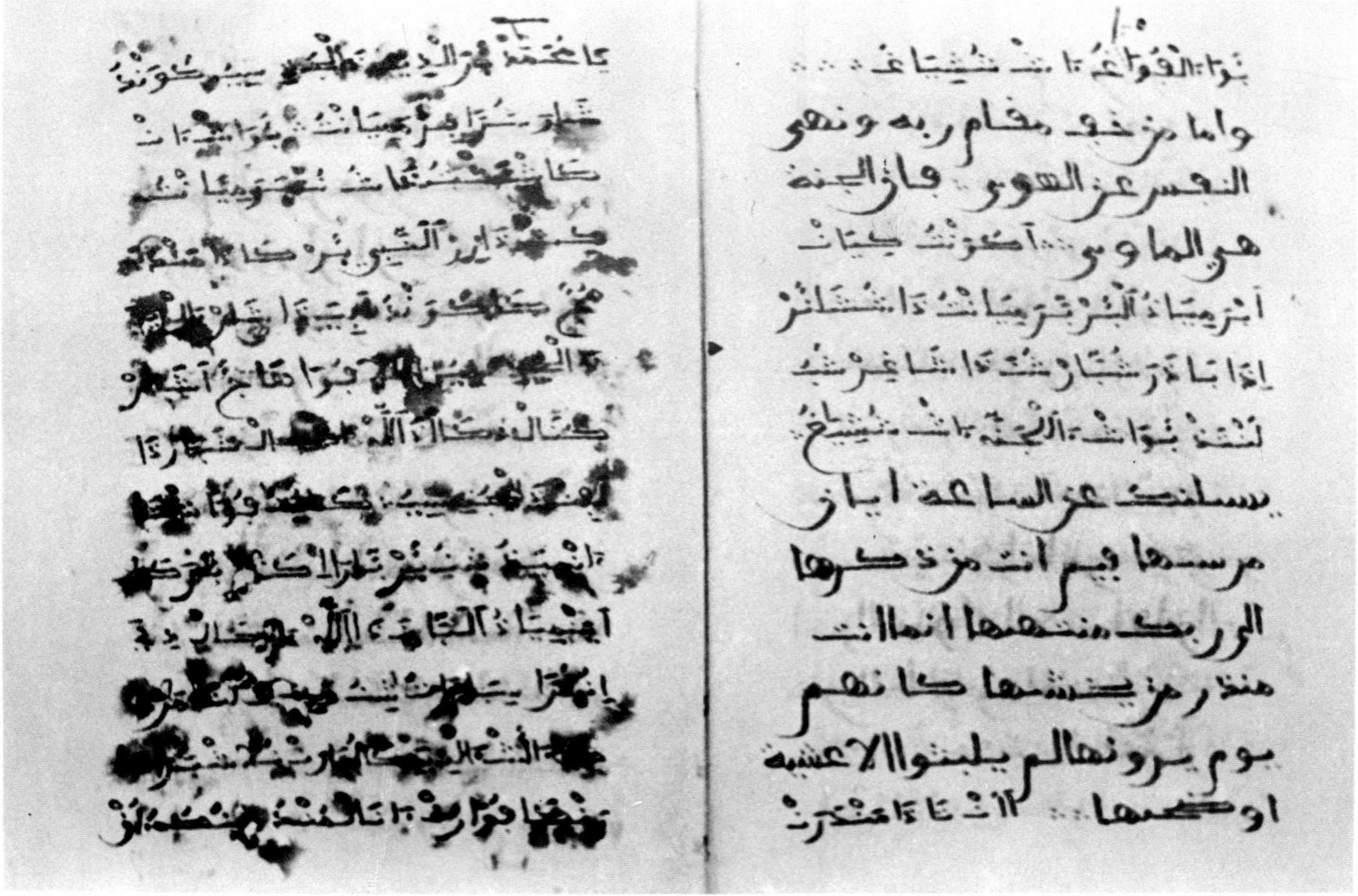

20: J 39, 101v-102r.

21 : BN 4938, 20v-21r.

22: BN 4938, 21v-22r.

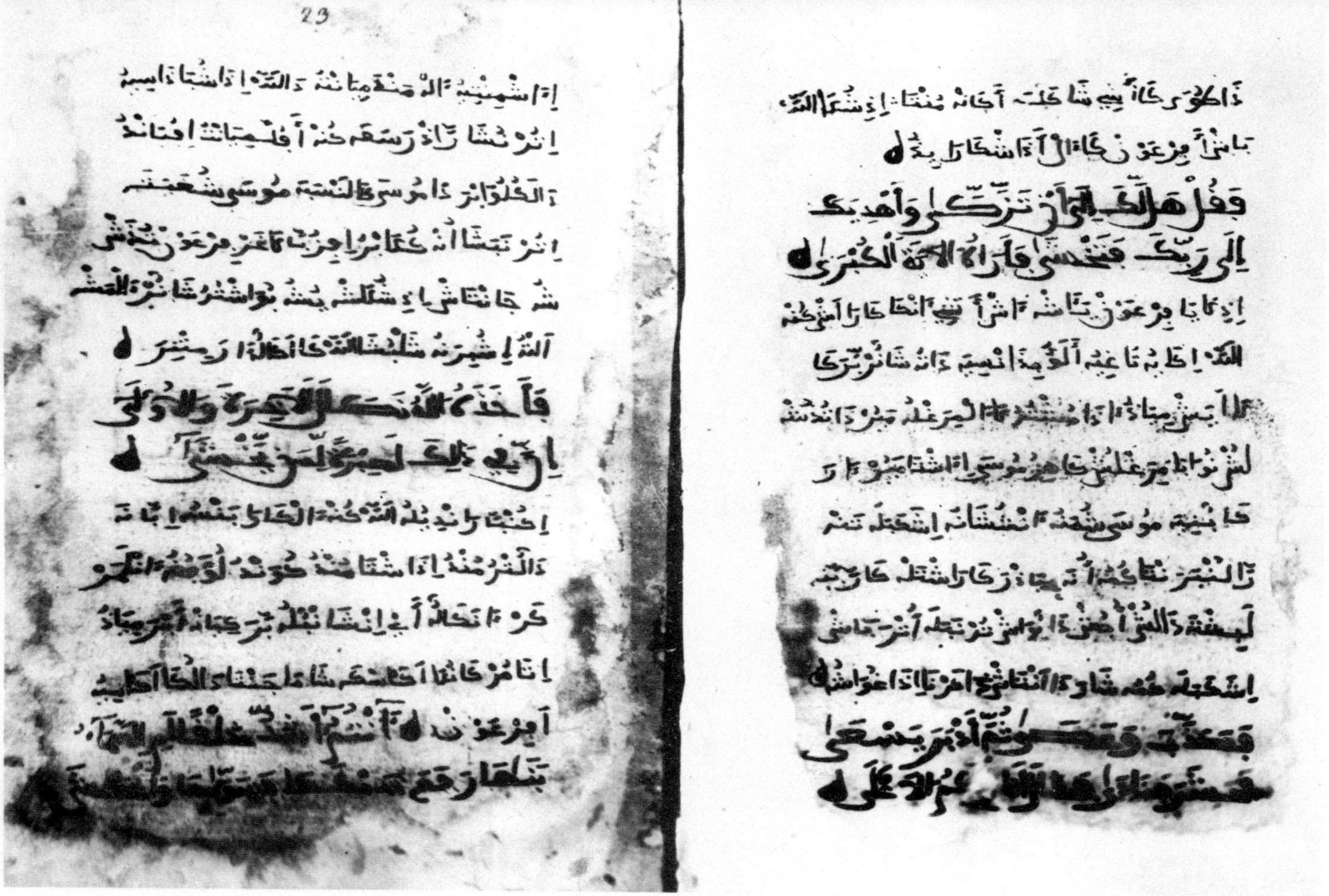

23: BN 4938, 22v-23r.

24: BN 4938, 23v-24r.

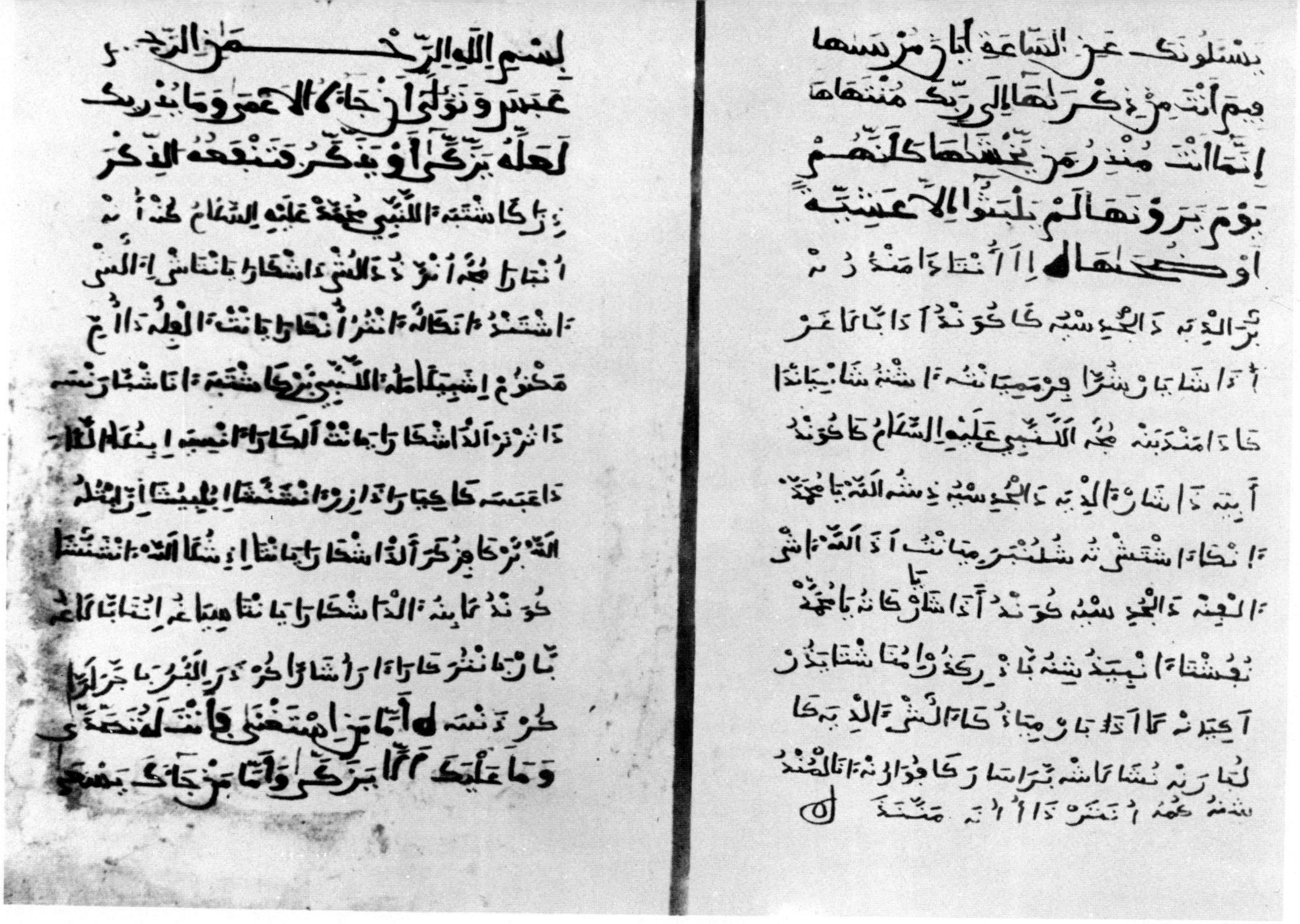

25: BN 4938, 24v-25r.

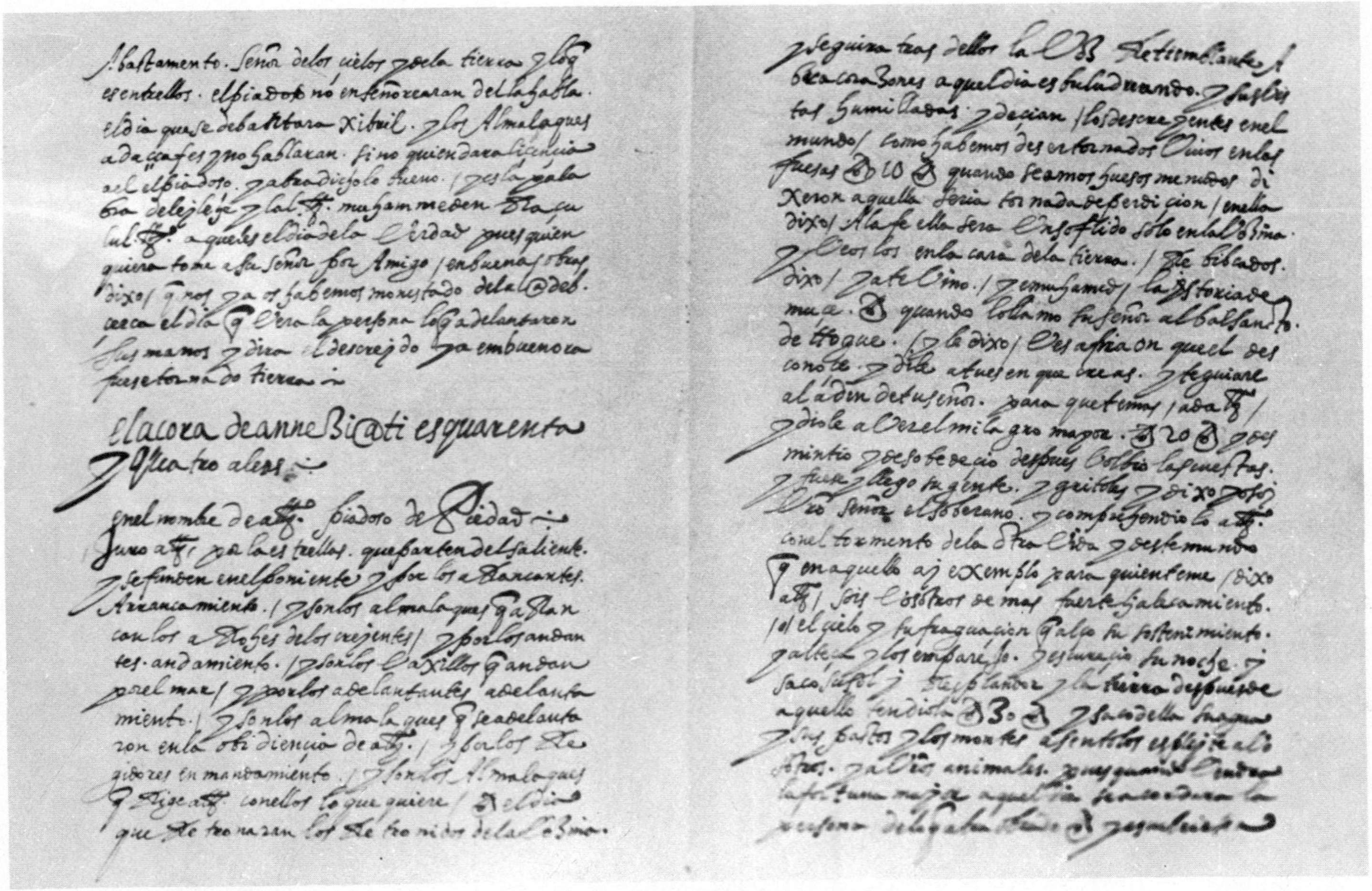

26: T 235, 335v-336r.

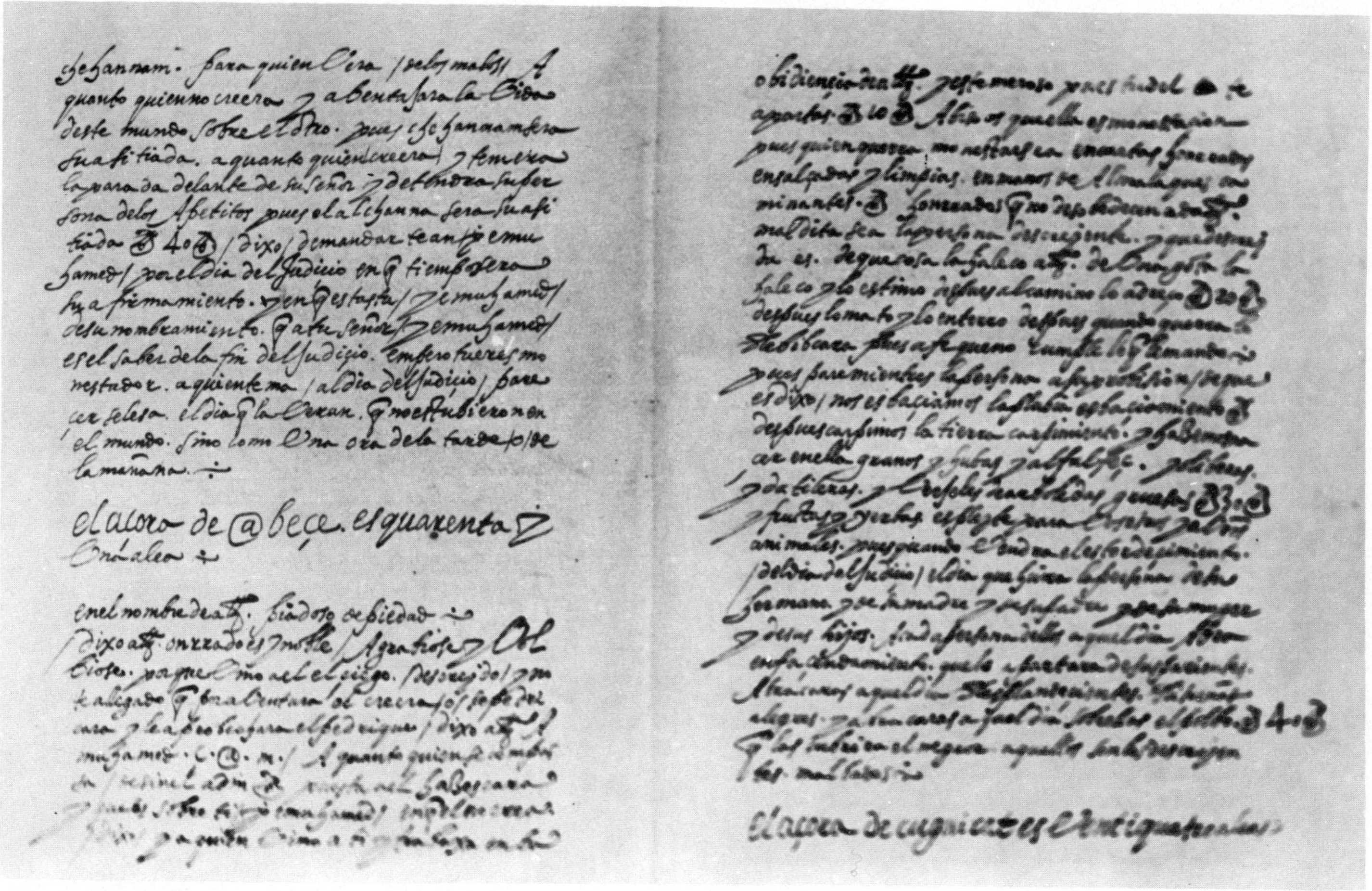

27: T 235, 336v-337r.

VII. Bibliography and abbreviations.

ᶜAbd al-Bāqī, M. F., *Al-muᶜjam al-mufahras li-alfāẓ al-qur'ān al-karīm,* 2nd ed. (Cairo, 1968).
Abū Ḥayyān al-Gharnāṭī, *Al-baḥr al-muḥīṭ fī tafsīr al-qur'ān,* 8 vols. (Cairo, 1328 A. H. [= 1910-11 A. D.]).
Actas = *Actas del Coloquio Internacional sobre Literatura Aljamiada y Morisca,* Colección de Literatura Española Aljamiado-Morisca, III (Madrid, 1978).
Actes Strasbourg = *Actes du Xᵉ Congrès International de Linguistique et Philologie Romanes* [Strasbourg, 1962], 3 vols. (Paris, 1965).
AFA = *Archivo de Filología Aragonesa.*
Al-Bayḍāwī, *Anwār at-tanzīl wa-asrār at-ta'wīl,* 4 vols. (Cairo, 1330 A. H. [= 1911-12 A. D.]).
Alcover, A. M., and F. de B. Moll, *Diccionari català-valencià-balear,* 10 vols. (Palma de Mallorca, 1930-60).
Alex. = *El libro de Alexandre,* ed. R. S. Willis, Jr., Elliott Monographs, XXXII (Princeton-Paris, 1934).
Alj. T.: see Kontzi.
Al-Qurṭubī, *Jāmiᶜ li-ahkām al-qur'ān,* 19 vols. (Cairo, 1967).
Alvar, *Dial.* = M. Alvar, *El dialecto aragonés* (Madrid, 1953).
Alvar, *T. dial.* = M. Alvar, *Textos hispánicos dialectales; antología histórica,* 2 vols. (Madrid, 1960).
Alverny, M.-T. d', "Deux traductions latines du Coran au Moyen Age", *Archives d'histoire doctrinale et littéraire du Moyen Age,* XXIII (1948), 69-131.
And = *Al-Andalus.*
Arberry, A. J., *The Koran Interpreted,* 2 vols. (London, 1955).
Ar-Rāzī, Fakhr ad-Dīn, *At-tafsīr al-kabīr,* ed. at-Tizām ᶜAbd ar-Raḥmān Muḥammad, 32 vols. (Cairo, 1934).
Aṭ-Ṭabarī, *Jāmiᶜ al-bayān fī tafsīr al-qur'ān,* 30 vols. (Būlāq, 1323-30 A. H. [= 1905-12 A. D.]).
Az-Zamakhasharī, *Al-kashshaf ᶜan haqā'iq at-tanzīl,* 3 vols. (Cairo, 1948).
Badía, *Bielsa* = A. Badía Margarit, *El habla del Valle de Bielsa* (Zaragoza, 1950).
Batallas: see Galmés.
Battisti, C., and G. Alessio, *Dizionario etimologico italiano,* 5 vols. (Florence, 1950-57).
BH = *Bulletin Hispanique.*
BICC = *Boletín del Instituto Caro y Cuervo.*
Boggs, R. S., et al., *A Tentative Dictionary of Medieval Spanish* (Chapel Hill, 1946).
Borao, G., *Diccionario de voces aragonesas,* 2nd ed. (Zaragoza, 1908).
Boronat y Barrachina, P., *Los moriscos españoles y su expulsión* (Valencia, 1901).
BRABLB = *Boletín de la Real Academia de Buenas Letras de Barcelona.*
Cabanelas, D., "Juan de Segovia y el primer Alcorán trilingüe", *And,* XIV (1949), 149-173.
———, *Juan de Segovia y el problema islámico* (Madrid, 1952).
Cattenoz, H. G., *Tables de concordance des ères chrétienne et hégirienne,* 3rd ed. (Rabat, 1961).
Craddock, J. R., "Concerning the Transliteration of Aljamiado Texts", *La Corónica,* IV (1976), 90-91.
DCELC = J. Corominas, *Diccionario crítico etimológico de la lengua castellana,* 4 vols. (Madrid-Bern, 1954-57).
DCR = R. J. Cuervo, *Diccionario de construcción y régimen de la lengua castellana,* 2 vols. [A-D] (Paris, 1886-93).
Derenbourg, H., *Les manuscrits arabes de l'Escurial* (Paris, 1884).
Dial.: see Alvar.
Dicc. Aut. = Real Academia Española, *Diccionario de la lengua española* ("*Diccionario de Autoridades*"), 3 vols. (Madrid, 1726-39; facsimile ed., 1963).
Diez, F., *Grammatik der romanischen Sprachen,* 5th ed. (Bonn, 1882).

Domínguez Ortiz, A., and B. Vincent, *Historia de los moriscos: vida y tragedia de una minoría* (Madrid, 1978).
EI = *The Encyclopaedia of Islam,* ed. M. T. Houtsma, T. W. Arnold, R. Basset, and R. Hartmann, 4 vols. Leiden-London, 1913-34, Supplement 1938); new ed., ed. H. A. Gibb et al., 4 vols. A-KH (1960-).
F. Arag. = G. Tilander, *Los fueros de Aragón según el manuscrito 458 de la Biblioteca Nacional de Madrid* (Lund, 1937).
Fernández de Heredia, J., *La Grant Crónica de Espanya,* I-II, ed. R. af Geijerstam, Studia Romanica Upsaliensia, 2 (Uppsala, 1964).
F. Teruel = *El Fuero de Teruel,* ed. M. Gorosch, Leges Hispanicae Medii Aevi, I (Stockholm, 1950).
GAL = C. Brockelmann, *Geschichte der arabischen Literatur,* 2nd ed., 2 vols. (Leiden, 1943-49), 3 Supplements (1937, 1938, 1942).
Galmés, *Batallas* = A. Galmés de Fuentes, *El libro de las batallas: Narraciones épico-caballerescas,* Colección de Literatura Española Aljamiado-Morisca, II, 2 vols. (Madrid, 1975).
——, *Influencias* = A. Galmés de Fuentes, *Influencias sintácticas y estilísticas del árabe en la prosa medieval castellana* (Madrid, 1956). Repr. from *BRAE,* XXXV (1955), 213-275, 415-451; XXXVI (1956), 65-131, 255-307.
——, *París* = A. Galmés de Fuentes, *Historia de los amores de París y Viana,* Colección de Literatura Española Aljamiado-Morisca, I (Madrid, 1970).
García de Diego, V., "Caracteres fundamentales del dialecto aragonés", *Miscelánea Filológica* (Zaragoza, 1919), 1-18.
Gifford, D. J., and F. W. Hodcroft, *Textos lingüísticos del medioevo español,* 2nd ed. (Oxford, 1966).
Gil, P., J. Ribera, and M. Sánchez, *Colección de textos aljamiados* (Zaragoza, 1888).
Guillén Robles, F., *Catálogo de los manuscritos árabes existentes en la Biblioteca Nacional de Madrid* (Madrid, 1889).
Hanssen, F., *Estudios sobre la conjugación aragonesa,* Anales de la Universidad, XCIII (Santiago [Chile], 1896).
Harvey, L. P., *The Literary Culture of the Moriscos 1492-1609. A Study Based on the Extant Manuscripts in Arabic and Aljamía,* unpublished D. Phil. dissertation (Magdalen College, Oxford, 1958).
Hava, J. G., *Al-Faraid Arabic-English Dictionary* (Beirut, 1970).
HR = *Hispanic Review.*
Ibn ᶜAṭiyya al-Gharnāṭī, *Al-muḥarrar al-wajīz fī tafsīr al-kitāb al-ᶜazīz,* vol. 1 (Cairo, 1974).
Ice de Gebir [= ᶜĪsā ibn Jābir], *Suma de los principales mandamientos y devedamientos de la ley y çunna,* ed. P. de Gayangos, *Memorial Histórico Español,* V (Madrid, 1853).
Influencias: see Galmés.
IQ = Islamic Quarterly.
Janer, F., *Condición social de los moriscos de España* (Madrid, 1857).
JAOS = *Journal of the American Oriental Society.*
Jeffrey, A., *Materials for the History of the Text of the Qur'an* (Leiden, 1937).
Keniston, *Syntax* = H. Keniston, *The Syntax of Castilian Prose: The Sixteenth Century* (Chicago, 1937).
Klenk, *L. Yūsuf* = U. Klenk, *La Leyenda de Yūsuf, ein Aljamiadotext,* Beihefte zur Zeitschrift für Romanische Philologie, Band 134 (Tübingen, 1972).
Kontzi, *Alj. T.* = R. Kontzi, *Aljamiadotexte. Ausgabe mit einer Einleitung zur Sprache und Glossar,* 2 vols. (Wiesbaden, 1974).
Kuhn, A., "Der Hocharagonesische Dialekt", *RLiR,* XI (1935), 1-312 (repr. Leipzig, 1936).
Lane, E. W., *Arabic-English Lexicon,* 8 vols. (London, 1863-93; repr. New York, 1955-56).
Lea, H. C., *The Moriscos of Spain* (Philadelphia, 1901; repr. New York, 1968).
Levi dell Vida, G., "Manoscritti arabi di origine spagnole nella Biblioteca Vaticana", *Collectanea Vaticana in honorem Anselmi M. Card. Albareda,* II (Rome, 1962), 181-184.
Lg = *Language.*
Libro Verde = M. Alvar, "Noticia lingüística del Libro Verde de Aragón", *AFA,* II (1947), 59-92.
Longás, P., *Vida religiosa de los moriscos* (Madrid, 1915).
López-Morillas, C., "Etimologías escogidas del Corán aljamiado (Manuscrito 4938 de la Biblioteca Nacional de Madrid)", *Actas,* 365-371.
——, *Lexical and Etymological Studies in the Aljamiado Koran Based on Manuscript 4938 of the Biblioteca Nacional, Madrid,* unpublished Ph. D. dissertation (University of California, Berkeley, 1974).

———, "Trilingual Marginal Notes (Arabic, Aljamiado, and Spanish) in a Morisco Manuscript from Toledo", *JAOS,* forthcoming.
Losada Campo, T., *Estudios sobre Coranes aljamiados,* unpublished doctoral dissertation (University of Barcelona, 1975).
L. Regum = L. Cooper, *El Liber Regum. Estudio Lingüístico, AFA,* Anejo 5 (Zaragoza, 1960).
L. Yūsuf: see Klenk.
MacGuckin de Slane, W., *Catalogue des manuscrits arabes de la Bibliothèque Nationale* (Paris, 1883).
Menéndez Pidal, *Orígenes* = R. Menéndez Pidal, *Orígenes del español: Estado lingüístico de la Península Ibérica hasta el siglo XI,* 5th ed. (= *Obras,* VIII) (Madrid, 1964).
———, *P. Yúçuf* = R. Menéndez Pidal, *El Poema de Yúçuf, Materiales para su estudio,* Colección Filológica de la Universidad de Granada, I (Granada, 1952).
Meyer-Lübke, W., *Romanisches etymologisches Wörterbuch,* 3rd ed. (Heidelberg, 1930-35).
MLR = *Modern Language Review.*
MO = *Monde Oriental.*
Moreno, M. M., "È lecito ai musulmani tradurre il Corano?", *OM,* V (1925), 532-543.
MPh = *Modern Philology.*
MW = *Muslim World.*
Navarro, T., *Documentos lingüísticos del Alto Aragón,* Publicaciones del Centro de Estudios Hispánicos, IV (Syracuse, 1957).
Neira Martínez, J., "Los prefijos *es-, des-* en aragonés", *Archivum* (O), XIX (1969), 331-341.
Nöldeke, T., *Geschichte des Qorans,* 2nd ed. (Leipzig, 1909-38).
Nykl, *R. Ališ.* = A. R. Nykl, "Aljamiado Literature. El Rrekontamiʸento del Rrey Ališandᵉre", *RH,* LXXVII (1929), 409-611.
Oelschläger, V. R. B., *A Medieval Spanish Word-List* (Madison, 1940).
OM = *Oriente Moderno.*
Orígenes: see Menéndez Pidal.
París: see Galmés.
Pardo Asso, J., *Nuevo diccionario etimológico aragonés* (Zaragoza, 1938).
Pattison, D. G., *Early Spanish Suffixes: A Functional Study of the Principal Nominal Suffixes of Spanish up to 1300,* Publications of the Philological Society, XXVII (Oxford, 1975).
Penrice, J., *A Dictionary and Glossary of the Koran* (London, 1873; repr. New York, 1969).
PhQ = *Philological Quarterly.*
Pottier, B., "L'évolution de la langue aragonaise à la fin du moyen âge", *BH,* LIV (1952), 182-199.
P. Yúçuf: see Menéndez Pidal.
RABM = *Revista de Archivos, Bibliotecas y Museos.*
Rahbar, D., "Aspects of the Qur'ān Translation", *Babel,* IX (1963), 60-68.
R. Ališ.: see Nykl.
RFE = *Revista de Filología Española.*
RH = *Revue Hispanique.*
Ribera, J., and M. Asín, *Catálogo de los manuscritos árabes y aljamiados de la Biblioteca de la Junta* (Madrid, 1912).
RLiR = *Revue de Linguistique Romane.*
RPh = *Romance Philology.*
Saavedra, E., "Indice general de la literatura aljamiada", Appendix to *Discurso leído ante la Real Academia Española* (Madrid, 1878), repr. in *Memorias de la Real Academia Española,* VI (1889), 140-328.
Silvestre de Sacy, A. I., et al., *Notices et extraits des manuscrits de la Bibliothèque Nationale,* 41 vols. (Paris, 1787-1933).
StIsl = *Studia Islamica.*
Syntax: see Keniston.
T. Dial.: see Alvar.
Terés Sádaba, E., *Los manuscritos árabes de la Real Academia de la Historia. La "Colección Gayangos"* (Madrid, 1975).
Teza, E., "Di un compendio del Corano in espagnolo con lettere arabiche (manoscritto fiorentino)", *Rendiconti della Reale Accademia dei Lincei. Cl. di scienze morale, storiche e filologiche,* Series 4, no. 7 (1891), 81-88.
Tibawi, A. L.: "Is the Qur'ān Translatable? Early Muslim Opinion", *MW,* LII (1962), 4-16.
UCPL = *University of California Publications in Linguistics.*

Umphrey, G. W., "The Aragonese Dialect", *RH,* XXIV (1911), 5-45.
Vernet, J., "La exégesis musulmana tradicional en los Coranes aljamiados", *Actas,* 123-145.
———, "Traducciones moriscas de El Corán", *Der Orient in der Forschung. Festschrift für Otto Spies* (Wiesbaden, 1967), 686-705.
———, and C. López Lillo, "Un manuscrito morisco del Corán", *BRABLB,* XXXV (1973-74), 185-255.
———, and L. Moraleda, "Un Alcorán fragmentario en aljamiado", *BRABLB,* XXXIII (1969-70), 43-75.
Vidal = G. Tilander, *Vidal Mayor. Traducción aragonesa de la obra In excelsis dei thesauris de Vidal de Canellas,* 3 vols. (Lund, 1956).
Viscasillas Seguí, M. V., *Traducciones aljamiadas del Corán. Estudio lingüístico de unos fragmentos. Manuscrito 25 de la Escuela de Estudios Arabes de Madrid,* unpublished licenciate thesis (Universidad Autónoma de Barcelona, 1973).
Watt, W. M., *Bell's Introduction to the Qur'ān,* Islamic Surveys, 8 (Edinburgh, 1970).
———, *Companion to the Qur'ān* (London, 1967).
Zetterstéen, K. V., "Some Chapters of the Koran in Spanish Transliteration", *MO,* V (1911), 39-41.
Zwemer, S. M., "Translation of the Koran", *MW,* V (1915), 244-261.